the **complete** *series*

Baking treats

R&R PUBLICATIONS MARKETING PTY LTD

Published by
R&R Publications Marketing Pty Ltd
ABN 78 348 105 138
PO Box 254, Carlton North
Victoria 3054, Australia
Phone: (61 3) 9381 2199
Fax: (61 3) 9381 2689
Email: info@randrpublications.com.au
Website: www.randrpublications.com.au
Australia-wide toll-free: 1800 063 296

**Want to receive our newsletter? Go to our website
at www.randrpublications.com.au to subscribe**

The Complete Baking Treats Cookbook

Publisher: Anthony Carroll
Designer: Aisling Gallagher
Food Stylist: Elly Cavell, R&R Photostudio
Food Photography: Paul Nelson, Elly Cavell, R&R Photostudio
Food Economist: Amanda Luck
Recipe Development: R&R Test Kitchen
Introduction: Samantha Carroll
Proofreader: Stephen Jones

Cover recipe The Perfect Pavlova on page 94

Recipes on page 15, 19, 20, 23, 24, 32, 35, 40 and 43 were provided by Tamara Milstein: tamara@tamaraskitchen.com

ISBN 978-1-74022-733-9

Printed August 2011
Printed in China

Contents

Introduction 4

Breads 11

Cookies 45

Pies and tarts 69

Desserts 93

Cakes 115

Cheesecakes 127

Shortbreads 149

Slices and squares 167

Scones and buns 189

Muffins 211

Cupcakes 233

Introduction

Baking has been with us for thousands of years, originating with the ancient Babylonians. Their techniques for baking bread were adopted by the ancient Egyptians and ancient Greeks and, by Roman times, banqueting tables groaned under tasty pastries, tortes and doughnut-like breads.

Unlike other cooking methods that rely upon radiant heat, baking utilises the dry heat of convection which can also be achieved using hot ashes or stones. Many of the ancient bakers began by smothering dough in such heated materials or shaping paste onto a hot rock. But the baker's craft has really come into its own since developing into an oven-based cuisine.

With advances in modern ovenware, more and more baked treats that had formerly been the preserve of master bakers and caterers can be produced in the home. Nowadays, many modern homes include state-of-the-art catering ovens – but even the advent of the basic oven has allowed home cooks to add increasingly sophisticated baked goods to their repertoires.

For baby-boomers, the soufflé was a floaty, French dessert only ever attempted by the brave or foolhardy, so uncertain was the likelihood of a successful outcome. Now, modern cooks can bake with greater confidence, although it is advisable to get to know your own oven as heat can vary from one unit to another. The many available settings, such as fan-forced, can also affect baking time and result.

Instinctively, we feel that there is something comforting and earthy about anything that is home-baked. Perhaps it is because few cooked foods have the ability to transport us back to our childhoods like the smell of freshly baked goods. For many of us, baked treats are comfort foods, harking back to treats that Grandma used to make. Cupcakes, hot cross buns, brownies – each has the power to elicit fond memories of the past and lift our spirits in the present. They are a favourite among kids and adults alike. With this book, you have the power to create new baked favourites in your own house.

Breads

Almost every culture bakes some sort of bread. French boulangers are prolific bakers. They brought their highly enriched eggy brioche to the culinary table. And who could be without that much-loved buttery pastry, the croissant, not to mention the ubiquitous crusty French baguette. Similarly, an Indian curry is

virtually incomplete without a yoghurty naan bread to scoop it up with. The Middle East has brought us the pita bread, that fabulously versatile flatbread that is the mainstay of any dipping platter. Other less traditional breads include soda bread, herbed beer bread and Australian damper that is enjoyed with golden syrup.

Cookies

Shop-bought cookies cannot compare to cookies baked at home. Fresh-baked cookies are both crisp and moist, a dimension that cookies from a packet can seldom achieve. Bake a batch and keep them in an airtight container for snack breaks...that's if they last that long once the family smells these freshly baked treats! Try the delectable combination of peanut butter and honey cookies, keep some almond biscotti on hand to have with after-dinner coffees, and be sure to pack some pecan crispies in the kids' lunch boxes.

Pies and tarts

Savoury pies can make a satisfying and delicious meal or snack – from the substantial beef and mushroom pie to individual meat pies to delectable meat-filled Cornish pasties. And perhaps nothing could encapsulate English pub grub better than an Old English pork pie (washed down with a pint of stout). The versatility of a finely rolled, crumbly pastry also perfectly accommodates a sweet filling, such as fruit mince pies and spicy pumpkin pie. Of course, open-faced pies – tarts – are the perfect vehicle for a sweet filling: orange chocolate tarts, rhubarb and apple tart, raspberry and hazelnut tarts, and fresh fruit tartlets are all here for you to enjoy.

Desserts

You will dazzle your dinner party guests with unique desserts like pavlova, named because of its light texture for the Russian ballerina Ánna Pávlova. Or whip up our effortless rhubarb soufflé or bake the decadent brandied plum clafouti – either would be a sophisticated finale to any dinner. For something more home-style, try the humble apple and rhubarb crumble – perfect with cream or icecream.

Cakes

Cakes form a central part of virtually every event, but you can bake a cake with no excuse at all except for wanting to satisfy a sweet tooth. The classic Madeira cake and orange poppy seed cake are perennial favourites, while raspberry chocolate truffle cakes will bring a wow factor to your next afternoon tea. Why not put on a proper high tea with the spongey goodness of the Victoria sandwich cake, replete with jam and cream, as its centrepiece.

Cheesecakes

Cheesecakes need not only be plain cream cheese and a biscuit crust: try the zesty combinations of citrus in our orange and lime cheesecake or enjoy the tropical buzz of papaya and lime cheesecake. The chocolate and caramel cheesecake is likely to become a family dessert mainstay and the mini passionfruit cheesecakes will give cupcakes a run for their money with the kids. For more mature tastes, try the plum and bitter orange cheesecake or the adults-only sultana and bourbon cheesecake.

Shortbreads

Shortbreads come in a much wider variety of flavours and shapes than you may expect. From the strawberry shortbread fan to the traditional Greek shortbread, they are the perfect Christmas gift that is gratefully received the whole year round.

Slices and squares

It is so easy to whip up slices or squares. You can keep them in a container in the fridge for when unexpected guests drop by. They will impress visitors in a way that a packet of cookies never can. The kids will love the lamingtons and caramel squares while the older folks won't be able to stop at one chocolate rum slice or the almond-flavoured marzipan triangles.

Scones and buns

Steep some tea, whip some cream and scoop some of your favourite jam into a dish. All that remains is to make a batch of our simple scone recipe and you have put together a Devonshire tea to rival any tea room. Some scone aficionados never go past plain scones with jam and cream, however there are a range of fabulous scone varieties you can experiment with in this book. Scones with currants, apple, ginger, dates, honey, even cheese. This is not to mention the scone's cousin, the hot cross bun, which is surprisingly easy to bake any time of year.

Muffins

Muffins are generally larger than cupcakes and can even substitute for them. They can be as sweet and satisfying as raspberry muffins or as buttery as peanut

butter muffins. They can also stand in for cereal as a breakfast on the run. Muffins lend themselves to the use of different grains such as wholemeal flour and oat bran, as well as dried fruits like raisins and dates – both of which encourage intestinal health.

Cupcakes

Holding a kids' party? There is no better way to entertain a group of children than by baking a batch of cupcakes and getting the kids to ice them themselves. Set up a table of different frostings and decorations and let them loose! It is both an involving activity and one that guarantees a yummy finale. It is also something you can do at home—better yet, involve your kids in the baking process. It will become a lifelong memory for all of you.

The reason for the continued popularity of home-baking is twofold: the creative satisfaction of making baked goods yourself is difficult to beat; it is also a form of culinary generosity. Cooking food for others is an act of love and, with baking in particular, a little love is baked into every bite! Baking is sharing that love. It is no coincidence that the nurturing act of growing a baby is known colloquially as having 'a bun in the oven'.

breads

They say that the best way to sell a house is to bake bread. A house filled with the smell of a freshly baked loaf on the day of the inspection instantly converts a house into a home. The crunchy crust and soft, pillowy interior of a buttery slice of bread fresh from the oven is something that a shop-bought loaf simply cannot match.

Naan bread

1 cup natural yoghurt
2 cups plain flour
3 cups stoneground wholemeal plain flour
1 tablespoon yeast
2 teaspoons salt
1 teaspoon sugar
2 tablespoons nut oil
3 tablespoons black sesame seeds
6 tablespoons sesame seeds

1 Preheat oven to 440°F/230°C.

2 Mix yoghurt with 1½ cups boiling water and stir well. Set aside for 5 minutes.

3 Mix plain flour with 1 cup of wholemeal flour and add yeast. Add yoghurt mixture and stir with a wooden spoon for 3 minutes, then cover with cling wrap. Allow to rest for 1 hour.

4 Add salt, sugar, oil and black sesame seeds and enough of the remaining flour to form a firm but moist dough. Begin to knead on a floured surface and continue until dough is very silky and elastic. Allow dough to rise in an oiled bowl for 1 hour at room temperature or until doubled in size.

5 Punch down dough and divide into 8 pieces. Shape each into a ball then flatten each piece of dough into a rough circle about ½ in/12mm thick. Transfer to oiled oven trays.

6 Brush surface of dough with water and sprinkle surface generously with sesame seeds.

7 Cover dough and allow to rise for 10 minutes. Bake for 5–8 minutes.

Serves 4 • Preparation 2½ hours • Cooking 8 minutes

Country cornbread

1 cup cornmeal
1 cup plain flour
2 tablespoons sugar
1 tablespoon baking powder
½ teaspoon salt
¾ cup milk
½ cup sour cream
2 eggs
3½ oz/100g butter, melted

1 Preheat oven to 350°F/180°C.
2 In a large mixing bowl, stir together all the dry ingredients. Mix the milk, cream, eggs and butter separately and blend well. Mix with the flour mixture until just combined.
3 Pour the batter into a well-oiled square cake tin, about 9 x 9 in/23 x 23cm. Bake for approximately 30 minutes until a skewer inserted into the bread comes out clean. Cut into squares or rectangles and serve warm.

Cornbread is a deliciously soft bread, served cut into squares and most commonly eaten with savoury dishes like chilli con carne and casseroles that have a gravy. It has been very popular in America for centuries, often eaten for breakfast with eggs and sausages. This recipe is an updated version, with sour cream included for extra richness.

Serves 8 • Preparation 15 minutes • Cooking 30 minutes

Soda bread

1 lb/500g plain flour
1 teaspoon baking soda
1 teaspoon salt
1½ oz/45g butter
2 cups buttermilk or milk

1 Preheat oven to 400°F/200°C.
2 Sift the flour, baking soda and salt into a bowl. Rub in the butter, using your fingertips, until the mixture resembles coarse breadcrumbs. Make a well in the centre of the flour mixture, pour in the milk or buttermilk and, using a round-ended knife, mix to form a soft dough.
3 Turn dough onto a floured surface and knead lightly until smooth. Shape into an 7 in/18cm round and place on a buttered and floured baking tray. Score dough into eighths using a sharp knife. Dust lightly with flour and bake for 35–40 minutes or until the loaf sounds hollow when tapped on the base.

Serves 8 • Preparation 15 minutes • Cooking 40 minutes

Basil beer bread

2 cups self-raising flour, sifted
2 oz/60g sugar
¾ cup fresh basil, chopped
1 teaspoon crushed black peppercorns
1 cup beer, at room temperature

1 Preheat oven to 350°F/180°C.
2 Place flour, sugar, basil, peppercorns and beer in a bowl and mix to make a soft dough.
3 Place dough in a buttered and lined 4 x 8 in/11 x 21cm loaf tin and bake for 50 minutes or until bread is cooked when tested with a skewer.
4 Stand bread in the tin for 5 minutes before turning onto a wire rack to cool. Serve warm or cold.

This bread is delicious spread with olive or sun-dried tomato paste. Any beer may be used; you can experiment with light and dark ales and even stout to achieve different results.

Makes one loaf • Preparation 15 minutes • Cooking 50 minutes

Croissants

7–8 cups unbleached bread flour
1 level tablespoon malt extract
4 tablespoons sugar
2 teaspoons salt

2 tablespoons yeast
2 tablespoons evaporated milk
1 lb/500g unsalted butter, chilled

1 Place flour, malt extract, sugar, salt, yeast, milk and 2 tablespoons of warm water in a mixing bowl and combine with a wooden spoon. When ingredients begin to stick together, turn out mass of dough and knead mixture gently on a well-floured surface until all ingredients are incorporated and dough is smooth and elastic (about 10 minutes). Shape into a rough square, flour well and place on a flat oven tray, covered loosely with cling wrap. Place in refrigerator for a minimum of 2 hours, or overnight.

2 When chilled, remove dough from refrigerator and roll out to a rectangular shape approximately 12 x 24 in/30 x 60cm. Using a vegetable peeler or cheese slicer, cut slices of chilled butter and lay them on bottom two thirds of dough.

3 Carefully seal seam, turn dough so seam is at the side and gently but firmly roll out dough to a large rectangle. Fold dough as before, bringing top third down and the bottom third up, then flour well and place on tray and chill for at least 2 hours. Repeat the above rolling, buttering, folding and rolling process again, using remaining butter. Again, chill for a minimum of 2 hours.

4 When ready to shape croissants, flour bench well. Firmly, but gently, roll out dough to a thickness of about ⅛ in/3mm and about 24 x 16 in/60 x 40cm. With a sharp knife, cut dough in half so that you have two pieces each 24 x 8 in/60 x 20cm.

5 Mark out triangles with base of about 3 in/8cm and height of 8 in/20cm so that full width of dough is used and each triangle joins the one before, with no wastage. Cut out these triangles. Place a small cut in middle of base of each triangle then roll triangles up gently but firmly, from base towards point of triangle. Continue rolling croissants up to form croissant shape and place them on an oiled oven tray, making sure that point lies under the croissant.

6 Gently curve corners to resemble a croissant. Allow to rise until doubled in size and carefully glaze with milk. Allow to rest for 30 minutes. Preheat oven to 460°F/240°C, then bake for approximately 10 minutes, watching for signs of burning. When baked, allow to cool on wire rack.

Serves 6 • Preparation 8 hours • Cooking 30 minutes

French olive ladder bread

1 tablespoon yeast
4 cups bread flour
2 cups wholemeal flour
¼ cup buckwheat flour
2 tablespoons olive oil
2 teaspoons sea salt
1–2 cups black olives, chopped

1 Preheat oven to 400°F/200°C.
2 Combine yeast, 3 cups warm water and 2 cups of bread flour and mix well with a wooden spoon for 3 minutes, until mixture resembles a thick batter. Cover with cling wrap and allow to rest for 2–3 hours at room temperature.
3 Add all remaining ingredients and mix to form a soft dough. Turn out onto a floured bench and knead well for about 10 minutes, adding a little extra flour if dough is too sticky. Return dough to an oiled bowl and allow to rise once more for 1 hour.
4 Remove dough from bowl and divide into four even pieces. Working with one piece at a time, flatten dough to a thickness of ½ in/12mm and approximately 12 x 4 in/ 30 x 10cm. With a sharp knife, make deep cuts in dough ½ in/12mm inside each edge and extending from one side of dough to other. When you have made four cuts, gently pull top and bottom of dough to stretch cuts, making cuts look like rungs on a ladder. Complete other pieces of dough in same manner. Transfer breads to oiled baking trays and allow to rise for 30 minutes at room temperature. Brush with olive oil and scatter a little sea salt over surface.
5 Bake for 20–25 minutes, until loaves are crisp and golden.

Serves 6 • Preparation 4 hours • Cooking 25 minutes

French baguettes

1 tablespoon dried yeast
1 tablespoon sugar
1 tablespoon salt
5–6 cups unbleached bread flour
1 egg white, beaten

1 Preheat oven to 430°F/220°C.

2 Mix yeast, sugar, salt and 4 cups of flour with 2 cups warm water. Add remaining flour, half a cup at a time, until dough is very soft but still manageable enough to knead. Turn dough out onto a floured surface and incorporate only as much flour as is needed to prevent sticking, then knead very well until dough is soft and satiny. Place in oiled bowl and allow to rise until doubled in size (about 2 hours). If you have time, this dough would benefit from a longer rise.

3 Turn dough out and cut into three or four equal portions (depending on required size of baguettes). Roll dough out to an oval shape and roll up tightly, Swiss-roll fashion. Roll shaped dough back and forth to lengthen baguette.

4 Brush surface with beaten egg white or water then sprinkle with flour. With a very sharp knife, slash tops of baguettes diagonally at 4 in/10cm intervals and allow dough to rise at room temperature until doubled in size (about 30 minutes). Bake for 20–30 minutes until crisp and pale golden.

Serves 4 • Preparation 3 hours • Cooking 30 minutes

Wholemeal damper

1 cup wholemeal self-raising flour
1 cup white self-raising flour
1¼ cups skim milk
1 teaspoon dry mustard
1 tablespoon sesame seeds

1 Prehat oven to 400°F/200°C.
2 Sift flour into a bowl, return husks from sifter to bowl. Stir in enough skim milk to give a sticky dough. Knead on lightly floured surface until smooth, shape into a round.
3 Place dough onto lightly buttered oven tray, press out with fingers to about 1 in/25mm thick. Using a sharp knife, mark into wedges, cut wedges into dough about ½ in/12mm deep.
4 Sprinkle dough with combined mustard and sesame seeds. Bake for 30 minutes or until golden brown and damper sounds hollow when tapped with fingers.

Makes one loaf • Preparation 20 minutes • Cooking 30 minutes

Pide

3⅓ cups plain flour
¼ oz/7g dry yeast
pinch of salt
1 teaspoon sugar
2 tablespoons olive oil
1 egg, lightly beaten
⅓ cup sesame seeds

1 Preheat oven to 440°F/220°C.
2 Combine flour, yeast, salt and sugar in a bowl. Make a well in the centre. Stir in 1½ cups warm water and oil. Mix to make a soft dough. Knead on a lightly floured surface for 10 minutes, adding more flour as needed, until soft, elastic and smooth. Place in a lightly oiled bowl. Turn to coat with oil. Cover. Stand in a warm place for 1 hour or until doubled in size.
3 Punch down. Divide into two equal portions. Roll each portion into a ball. Cover with tea towel. Stand in a warm place for 20–30 minutes.
4 Flatten each ball to make a 10 in/25cm circle. Pull into an oval shape. Place on a lightly buttered baking tray. Make indentations over surface with fingertips, leaving a 1 in/25mm border. Brush generously with egg. Sprinkle with sesame seeds.
5 Bake for 15 minutes or until golden. Wrap in a tea towel. Cool.

Makes 18 pieces • Preparation 2 hours • Cooking 15 minutes

Herbed beer bread

2 cups plain flour
1 teaspoon baking soda
1½ oz/45g Parmesan cheese, grated
2 tablespoons pitted black olives, chopped
2 tablespoons olive oil
¾ cup beer
¾ cup chopped mixed fresh herbs, for example, parsley, basil, coriander and oregano

1 Preheat oven to 360°F/180°C.
2 Combine flour, baking soda, Parmesan cheese and olives in a bowl. Make a well in the centre. Mix in oil and enough beer to make a moist dough.
3 Spoon one third of the dough into a buttered 3 x 8 in/8 x 20cm loaf tin. Sprinkle with one half of the herbs. Top with one third of the remaining dough. Sprinkle with remaining herbs. Top with remaining dough. Brush with a little milk.
4 Bake for 1 hour or until base sounds hollow when tapped.

Makes 16 slices • Preparation 20 minutes • Cooking 1 hour

Coconut poori

1 cup wholemeal flour (or Indian atta flour)
½ cup plain flour
½–1 teaspoon salt
3½ oz/100g desiccated coconut
1 teaspoon chilli powder
½ tablespoon sugar
2 tablespoons ghee or vegetable oil

1 Mix wholemeal flour, plain flour, salt and coconut in a bowl with chilli powder and sugar. Add melted ghee or oil and rub through until flour appears crumbly. Stir in about ½ cup water, only add water as much as necessary to form a soft dough. Knead dough well. Allow the dough to rest for 10 minutes.

2 Divide the dough into 14 pieces, flattening each and rolling each out to a thin circle of 3 in/8cm diameter.

3 Heat oil in a wok and, when hot, add one circle of dough. With a heat-proof implement, push dough under oil until dough is puffed and golden. Allow it to float, turning to cook the other side.

4 Drain on absorbent paper and cook remaining poori the same way.

Poori are one of the most popular breads in India. These puffed-up pillow-style breads are fun to make and taste delicious.

Makes 14 poori • Preparation 30 minutes • Cooking 30 minutes

Potato naan

1 cup natural yoghurt
2 cups plain flour
3 cups stoneground wholemeal flour
1 tablespoon yeast
2 teaspoons salt
1 teaspoon sugar
2 tablespoons peanut oil
3 tablespoons black sesame seeds
1 egg, beaten

Filling
1 lb/500g potatoes, peeled and diced
1 onion, finely diced
4 mint leaves, finely sliced
¼ cup parsley, chopped
½ cup coriander leaves, chopped
¼ teaspoon ground cumin
¼ teaspoon ground turmeric
salt and freshly ground black pepper

1 Preheat oven to 400°F/200°C.

2 Mix yoghurt with 1½ cups boiling water and stir well. Set aside for 5 minutes.

3 Mix plain flour with 1 cup of wholemeal flour and add yeast. Add yoghurt mixture and stir with a wooden spoon for 3 minutes then allow to rest for 30 minutes.

4 Add salt, sugar, oil and black sesame seeds and enough of the remaining flour to form a firm but moist dough.

5 Begin to knead on a floured surface and continue until dough is very silky and elastic. Allow dough to rest in an oiled bowl for 1 hour or until doubled in size.

6 Meanwhile make potato filling. Cover potatoes, and boil until soft. Mix hot potato with onion, mint leaves, parsley, coriander, cumin, turmeric and salt and pepper and mash until soft but not sloppy. Cool.

7 Punch down dough and divide into 12 equal pieces. Roll each piece into a circle about 5 in/15cm in diameter. Place a large tablespoon of filling in the centre of each dough circle and lift both edges of circle to seal. Pinch seam together very well. Allow to rise for 10 minutes then brush with beaten egg and sprinkle with sesame seeds. Bake for 15–20 minutes or until golden and crisp.

Serves 4 • Preparation 2 hours • Cooking 20 minutes

Chapatis

250g wholemeal flour
1 teaspoon salt

1 Sift flour and salt into a bowl. Make a well in the centre and add 1 cup of water, a little at a time, using your fingers to incorporate the surrounding flour to make a smooth, pliable dough.

2 Knead dough on a lightly floured surface for 5–10 minutes, then place in a bowl, cover with a cloth and leave to rest for 30–60 minutes.

3 Knead dough for 2–3 minutes. Divide into 6 balls of equal size, then flatten each ball a circle, about 5 in/12cm in diameter.

4 Heat an unbuttered frying pan until hot. Place one chapati at a time on hot surface. As soon as bubbles appear on surface of chapati, turn the chapati over. Press down on chapati with a thick cloth so that it cooks evenly.

5 To finish chapati, lift it with a fish slice and hold it carefully over an open gas flame without turning until it puffs up slightly. Alternatively, place the chapati under a hot grill.

6 Repeat with remaining dough circles. Keep cooked chapatis hot in a covered napkin-lined basket.

Makes 15 • Preparation 1 hour • Cooking 30 minutes

Holiday spice bread

1 oz/30g unsalted butter, melted
1 cup almonds, coarsely chopped
½ cup sultanas
¼ teaspoon salt
¼ teaspoon nutmeg
1 teaspoon ground ginger
1½ teaspoon ground cinnamon
1 teaspoon anise seed
pinch of ground cloves
1½ teaspoon dried orange peel, minced
1 teaspoon baking powder

2 teaspoons baking soda
1 cup honey
¼ cup brown sugar
1 large egg, lightly beaten
⅓ cup dark rum
1 cup rye flour
1 cup wholemeal flour
1 cup bread flour

1 Preheat oven to 400°F/200°C.

2 Butter one 8-cup loaf tin 6 x 10 in/15 x 25cm or two 4½ cup loaf tins 3 x 7 in/ 8 x 18cm. Dust bottom and sides with flour, shaking out excess.

3 In a large mixing bowl, combine almonds, sultanas, salt, nutmeg, ginger, cinnamon, anise seed, cloves, orange peel, baking powder and baking soda. Bring 1 cup water to a boil in a medium saucepan over moderate heat. Add honey and stir to dissolve. Add brown sugar and stir to dissolve. Remove from heat, allow to cool for 5 minutes.

4 Add egg and rum to honey and sugar mixture and whisk to blend. Add to spice mixture and stir to blend. Add flours and stir until flour is just absorbed (about 50 strokes). Transfer dough to prepared pan and bake for 10 minutes. Reduce heat to 360°F/180°C and bake until a cake tester inserted in centre comes out dry (about 30 more minutes for one large pan, 20–25 more minutes for smaller pans). Bread will be very dark.

5 Let bread cool in pan on a rack for 5 minutes. Remove from tin and finish cooling on rack. Wrap tightly with plastic wrap and store at room temperature for 2–3 days before serving. Thinly slice to serve.

Makes one loaf • Preparation 30 minutes • Cooking 40 minutes

French sourdough with caramelised onions

1 cup wholemeal flour
1 cup natural yoghurt
1 teaspoon sugar
1 teaspoon yeast
1½ oz/45g butter
4 large onions, sliced
1 tablespoon dried yeast
1 teaspoon sugar
1½ teaspoons salt
1 teaspoon baking soda
2–3 cups wholemeal flour

1 In a large mixing bowl, combine wholemeal flour, yoghurt, sugar, yeast and ¼ cup warm water. Mix well, then set aside and allow to ferment at room temperature for 24 hours.

2 The next day, melt butter in large frypan and add sliced onions. Stir to coat with butter and cook over medium heat until onions are translucent. Cover saucepan with lid and continue to cook on low heat for about 40 minutes or until onions are golden brown. Set aside to cool.

3 Mix yeast, ¼ cup warm water and sugar together and allow to sit for 5 minutes. Mix this mixture into prepared starter dough along with salt, half the caramelised onions and the baking soda. Slowly add more flour until dough forms a shaggy mass.

4 When dough is quite smooth and manageable, allow it to rise for 30 minutes at room temperature. Remove dough from bowl and divide in half. Shape each piece of dough into a flat oval loaf about ½ in/12mm thick, using your fingertips to add texture to dough. Scatter remaining onions over surface of dough then drizzle dough with some olive oil and allow to rest again for 30 minutes. Preheat oven to 400°F/200°C. Spray dough with water and bake for 25–30 minutes, or until crusty and golden.

Serves 6 • Preparation 1 hour, plus standing time • Cooking 30 minutes

Fougasse Provençale

2 cups bread flour
1 large tablespoon yeast
3 lb/1½ kg plain flour
1½ tablespoon salt
1 tablespoon yeast
8 cloves garlic, freshly minced
⅓ cup olive oil

1 To make starter, mix flour, yeast and water together until mixture resembles a semi-thick batter. Allow to prove, covered, in a non-reactive bowl for up to 3 days (8 hours minimum) to develop a lovely mature flavour.

2 To make dough, mix the starter, 1 kg of flour and salt, yeast, garlic and half the oil with 1 cup of warm water to make a soft dough. Knead on floured surface until dough is silky smooth, adding remaining flour as necessary until dough is no longer sticky. Allow dough to rise at room temperature in an oiled bowl until doubled in size (about 2 hours).

3 Divide dough into 12 pieces and, using your fingertips or rolling pin, shape into ovals about 1cm thick. With a sharp knife, make diagonal cuts through dough and then gently stretch to open up holes. Brush with remaining oil and sprinkle with a little sea salt if desired.

4 Preheat oven to 200°F/100°C. Allow dough to rise for 30 minutes at room temperature then bake for 15–20 minutes, spraying with water twice during baking (if you prefer, place baking pan of boiling water in bottom of oven to create steam). Remove from oven and brush once more with olive oil before cooling.

Serves 6 • Preparation 2½ hours, plus standing time • Cooking 20 minutes

cookies

What completes a coffee break or cup of tea better than a cookie? Called biscuits in the United Kingdom and Australasia, biscotti in Italy, cookies in North America, and a range of other names the world over, these small flat-baked snacks are also the classic after-school treat. The word cookie comes from the Dutch word koekje which means little cake and may include spices, nuts, fruit, peanut butter or chocolate.

Sweet cinnamon bows

4 oz/125g cream cheese
4 oz/125g unsalted butter
1½ cups plain flour
¼ cup caster sugar
2 teaspoons ground cinnamon
icing sugar, sifted

1 Roughly chop cream cheese and butter and set aside to stand at room temperature for 10 minutes. Place flour, sugar and cinnamon in a food processor and process briefly to sift. Add cream cheese and butter and process, using the pulse button, until mixture is combined. Take care not to overmix the dough. Turn dough onto a lightly floured surface, gather into a ball and knead briefly. Wrap dough in cling wrap and refrigerate for at least 1 hour.

2 Preheat oven to 380°F/190°C. Roll out dough to ⅛ in/3mm thick. Cut dough into strips ½ in/12mm wide and 8 in/20cm long, using a pastry wheel or sharp knife. Shape each strip into a bow and place on baking trays lined with non-stick baking paper. Cover and refrigerate for 15 minutes. Bake for 5 minutes, then reduce temperature to 300°F/150°C and cook for 10–15 minutes or until puffed and golden brown. Transfer to wire racks to cool. Store in airtight containers. Just prior to serving, sprinkle with icing sugar.

Makes 50 • Preparation 1½ hours • Cooking 20 minutes

Cinnamon cookies

8 oz/250g soft butter
4 oz/125g caster sugar
1 teaspoon vanilla extract
3 cups plain flour
2 teaspoons ground cinnamon
salt
1½ cups icing sugar

1 Butter two baking sheets. Beat together butter, sugar and vanilla extract. Stir in flour, 1 teaspoon cinnamon and a pinch of salt to make a soft dough. Cover and refrigerate for 1 hour.

2 Preheat oven to 360°F/180°C. Form mixture into 1 in/25mm balls and place on a prepared baking sheet, leaving space between each one. Bake for 15 minutes. Remove from oven, leave on baking sheets for a few minutes, then transfer to a wire rack to cool. Mix together icing sugar and remaining cinnamon and sieve over the cookies before serving.

Makes 24 • Preparation 1 hour • Cooking 15 minutes

Pecan crispies

3 egg whites
pinch of salt
1 teaspoon vanilla extract
¾ cup caster sugar
2 cups pecans, chopped

1 Preheat oven to 360°F/180°C.
2 Beat egg whites in a large bowl with an electric mixer until soft peaks form.
3 Add salt, vanilla and sugar, beat for a further 1 minute then fold in nuts.
4 Drop teaspoonfuls of mixture onto a baking-paper-lined baking tray.
5 Bake for 2–3 minutes, turn off oven and leave biscuits in oven for 60 minutes.
6 Use a spatula to ease biscuits off paper, store in an airtight container.

Makes about 72 • Preparation 15 minutes • Cooking 3 minutes, plus standing time

Oatmeal biscuits

4 oz/125g butter
1 cup brown sugar
2 eggs
2 ripe bananas, mashed
3 teaspoons vanilla extract
2½ cups plain flour
1½ cups rolled oats
½ teaspoon baking powder
½ cup chopped hazelnuts

1 Preheat oven to 360°F/180°C.
2 Cream butter and sugar using an electric mixer until fluffy. Add egg and beat well. Add banana and vanilla.
3 Combine flour, oats and baking powder in another bowl. Gradually, add the flour mixture and milk to banana mixture. Add hazelnuts.
4 Place tablespoons of mixture onto lightly buttered oven tray. Bake for 10 minutes or until slightly browned on edges. Cool on wire rack.

Makes about 40 • Preparation 20 minutes • Cooking 10 minutes

Almond biscotti

1⅔ cups plain flour
½ teaspoon baking powder
2 large eggs
½ cup caster sugar
1 teaspoon vanilla extract
1 teaspoon grated orange zest
¾ cup blanched almonds, lightly toasted
egg white

1 Preheat oven to 360°F/180°C.
2 Sift flour and baking powder into a bowl. In a separate bowl, beat eggs, sugar, vanilla extract and orange zest until thick and creamy. Fold egg mixture and almonds into flour mixture.
3 Knead on a floured surface to a firm dough. Divide dough in half. Shape each piece into a log about 2 in/50mm wide and 1 in/25mm thick. Place on a buttered and floured baking tray. Brush with egg white.
4 Bake for 30 minutes or until firm. Cool for 10 minutes. Cut each log diagonally into 1cm thick slices. Place on baking trays. Bake for 20–30 minutes or until dry and crisp. Cool on wire racks. Store in an airtight container.

Makes 30 slices • Preparation 20 minutes • Cooking 1 hour

Peanut butter and honey cookies

¾ cup crunchy peanut butter
⅔ cup honey
1 egg, lightly beaten
1 cup plain flour, sifted
½ cup rolled oats
⅓ cup sultanas

1 Preheat oven to 320°F/160°C.
2 Place peanut butter and honey in a saucepan. Cook, stirring, over low heat until soft and combined. Cool slightly. Stir in egg. Fold in remaining ingredients.
3 Shape teaspoons of mixture into balls. Place on paper-lined baking trays. Press lightly with a fork. Bake for 12 minutes or until golden. Cool on wire racks.

Makes 30 • Preparation 15 minutes • Cooking 12 minutes

Hazelnut macaroons

2 egg whites
½ cup icing sugar, sifted
1 cup ground hazelnuts
1 teaspoon finely grated orange zest
¼ cup flaked almonds

1 Preheat oven to 400°F/200°C.
2 Beat egg whites until soft peaks form. Combine remaining ingredients and fold into egg whites.
3 Place spoonfuls of mixture on paper-lined baking trays. Bake for 10–12 minutes or until golden. Cool on wire racks.

Makes 20 • Preparation 15 minutes • Cooking 12 minutes

Ginger biscuits

1 oz/30g butter
¼ cup sugar
1 egg
½ cup wholemeal plan flour, sifted
½ cup white plain flour, sifted
2 teaspoons ground ginger
1 tablespoon glacé ginger
½ teaspoon ground nutmeg
¼ teaspoon ground cloves
2 tablespoons molasses or golden syrup, warmed

1 Preheat oven to 320°F/160°C. Beat butter and sugar in a bowl until light and fluffy. Beat in egg. Stir in remaining ingredients. Cover and refrigerate for 1 hour.

2 Roll teaspoons of mixture into balls. Place on lightly buttered baking trays. Flatten slightly. Bake for 10–12 minutes or until golden.

Makes 28 • Preparation 1 hour • Cooking 12 minutes

Ginger snaps

1 cup brown sugar
3 teaspoons ground ginger
2 cups plain flour
3 oz/90g butter
1 cup golden syrup
1 teaspoon baking powder

1 Preheat the oven to 360°F/180°C.

2 Sift the sugar, ginger and flour together into a bowl.

3 Place the butter and golden syrup in a saucepan and cook over a low heat, stirring, until the butter melts. Stir in the baking powder. Pour the syrup mixture into the dry ingredients and mix until smooth.

4 Drop teaspoons of the mixture onto buttered baking trays and bake for 10–12 minutes or until golden. Remove from the oven, loosen the biscuits with a spatula, and allow to cool on trays.

Makes 45 • Preparation 20 minutes • Cooking 12 minutes

Butter cookies

4 oz/125g butter
4 oz/125g ghee
1¼ cups caster sugar
½ teaspoon ground cinnamon
3 eggs
⅓ cup brandy
1½ teaspoons baking powder
4–5 cups plain flour
sesame seeds

1 Preheat oven to 380°F/190°C.
2 Cream butter, ghee and sugar well, and add cinnamon. Gradually add eggs, beating mixture well.
3 Add brandy and baking powder, then begin to add flour. Add as much as is needed to make a stiff (not dry) dough. It is safer to add half the flour, then mix in a little at a time until desired consistency is reached. Test to see if dough is right by rolling a little in your hands – if it is not sticky, and rolls well, enough flour has been added.
4 Shape pieces of dough into slim pencil-shapes, roll in sesame seeds, then form into twists, circles or scrolls. Place on buttered baking sheet, glaze with egg glaze and bake for 15–20 minutes. Cool on wire rack.

Makes about 48 • Preparation 20 minutes • Cooking 20 minutes

Pistachio oat bran biscuits

2 oz/60g butter
⅔ cup sugar
1 teaspoon vanilla extract
½ teaspoon baking soda
½ teaspoon cream of tartar
1 cup plain flour
½ cup oat bran
⅓ cup buttermilk
½ cup chopped pistachios

1 Preheat oven to 400°F/200°C.

2 Combine butter and sugar in a bowl, beat until creamy. Add vanilla, baking soda and cream of tartar. Mix in well.

3 Combine four and oat bran, fold in alternately with buttermilk in three batches, mixing well after each addition. Fold in half the pistachios.

4 Roll teaspoons of the mixture and press into remaining pistachios. Place them pistachio-side up on a lightly buttered baking sheet. Bake until golden, about 10 minutes.

5 Remove baking sheet from oven, cool biscuits on sheet for 2 minutes. Remove biscuits to wire rack to cool completely. Store in an airtight container.

Makes about 30 • Preparation 20 minutes • Cooking 10 minutes

pies & tarts

What is a better cure for the winter blues (or a savoury treat the whole year round) than a meat pie and sauce? Savoury pies combine crispy and crumbly pastry with slow-cooked meat and silky gravy. Follow with a sweet tart, such as orange chocolate tart, fruit mince tarts or fresh fruit tartlets, and you have the perfect two-course meal!

Pear and fig flan

Hazelnut pastry
2 cups flour, sifted
1½ oz/45g finely chopped hazelnuts
1 teaspoon ground mixed spice
7 oz/200g butter, chilled and cut into small
  cubes
1 egg yolk, lightly beaten with a few drops
  vanilla extract

Pear and fig filling
4 pears, peeled, cored and quartered
3 oz/90g butter
4 oz/125g dried figs, chopped
½ cup brown sugar
½ cup golden syrup
½ teaspoon vanilla extract
½ cup plain flour
1 egg, lightly beaten

1 Preheat oven to 440°F/220°C. To make pastry, place flour, hazelnuts and mixed spice in a bowl, then using fingertips, rub in butter until mixture resembles fine breadcrumbs. Using a metal spatula or round-ended knife, mix in egg yolk mixture and enough chilled water (3–4 tablespoons) to form a soft dough. Turn dough onto a lightly floured surface and knead gently until smooth. Wrap dough in cling wrap and chill for 30 minutes.

2 On a lightly floured surface, roll out pastry and use to line a lightly buttered, deep 9 in/23cm flan tin. Chill for 15 minutes. Line pastry case with baking paper, fill with uncooked rice and bake for 10 minutes. Remove rice and paper and cook for 10 minutes more.

3 To make filling, cut each pear quarter into four slices. Melt 1½ oz/45g butter in a frying pan over a medium heat, add pears and cook for 4–5 minutes. Arrange pear slices in pastry case, then scatter with figs.

4 Place remaining butter, sugar, golden syrup, ½ cup water and the vanilla in a saucepan and cook over a medium heat until sugar dissolves. Bring to the boil and simmer for 2 minutes.

5 Remove pan from heat and set aside to cool for 15 minutes, then beat in flour and egg. Pour mixture over pears and figs and bake at 360°F/180°C for 50–55 minutes or until filling is firm.

Serves 8 • Preparation 1 hour • Cooking 1½ hours

Rhubarb and apple tart

Pastry
1 cup plain flour, sifted
2 teaspoons icing sugar, sifted
3 oz/90g butter, cubed

Rhubarb and apple filling
6 stalks rhubarb, chopped
2 tablespoons sugar
1 oz/30g butter
3 green apples, cored, peeled and sliced
4 oz/125g cream cheese
⅓ cup sugar
1 teaspoon vanilla extract
1 egg

1 Preheat oven to 400°F/200°C. To make pastry, place flour and icing sugar in a bowl and rub in butter, using your fingertips, until mixture resembles coarse breadcrumbs. Add 4 teaspoons iced water and knead to a smooth dough. Wrap in cling wrap and refrigerate for 30 minutes.

2 Roll out pastry on a lightly floured surface and line a buttered 9 in/23cm fluted flan tin with removable base. Line pastry case with non-stick baking paper and weigh down with uncooked rice. Bake for 15 minutes. Remove rice and paper and cook for 5 minutes longer.

3 To make filling, poach rhubarb until tender. Drain well, stir in sugar and set aside to cool. Melt butter in a frying pan and cook apples for 3–4 minutes. Remove apples from pan and set aside to cool.

4 Place cream cheese, sugar, vanilla extract and egg in a bowl and beat until smooth. Spoon rhubarb into pastry case, then top with cream cheese mixture and arrange apple slices attractively on top. Reduce oven temperature to 360°F/180°C and cook for 40–45 minutes or until filling is firm.

Serves 10 • Preparation 45 minutes • Cooking 1 hour 15 minutes

Raspberry and hazelnut tarts

1 cup flour, sifted
2 tablespoons icing sugar
1 oz/30g hazelnuts, ground
2½ oz/80g unsalted butter, chopped
1 egg, lightly beaten

Cream filling
13 oz/375g cream cheese
2 tablespoons caster sugar
¼ cup double cream

Raspberry topping
12 oz/350g raspberries
⅓ cup raspberry jam, warmed and sieved

1 To make pastry, place flour, icing sugar and hazelnuts in a bowl and mix to combine. Rub in butter, using fingertips, until mixture resembles fine breadcrumbs. Add egg and mix to form a soft dough. Wrap in cling wrap and refrigerate for 1 hour.

2 Preheat oven to 400°F/200°C. Knead pastry lightly, then roll out to ⅛ in/3mm thick and line six lightly buttered 3 in/75mm flan tins. Line pastry cases with baking paper and weigh down with uncooked rice and bake for 10 minutes. Remove paper and rice and bake for 15 minutes longer or until golden. Set aside to cool.

3 To make filling, place cream cheese and sugar in a bowl and beat until smooth. Beat cream until soft peaks form then fold into cream cheese mixture. Cover and chill for 20 minutes.

4 To assemble, spoon filling into pastry cases and smooth tops. Arrange raspberries over top of tarts, then brush warm jam over raspberries and refrigerate for a few minutes to set glaze.

Serves 6 • Preparation 40 minutes • Cooking 25 minutes

Spicy pumpkin pie

Pastry
1 cup flour
½ teaspoon baking powder
3½ oz/100g butter, cut into pieces
1½ tablespoon caster sugar
1 egg yolk

Spicy pumpkin filling
10 oz/300g pumpkin, cooked and puréed
2 eggs, lightly beaten
½ cup sour cream
½ cup double cream
¼ cup golden syrup
½ teaspoon ground nutmeg
½ teaspoon ground mixed spice
½ teaspoon ground cinnamon

1 Preheat oven to 400°F/200°C.
2 To make pastry, sift flour and baking powder into a mixing bowl. Rub in butter with fingertips until mixture resembles coarse breadcrumbs, then stir in sugar. Make a well in the centre and mix in egg yolk and ½–1 tablespoon water to mix to a firm dough. Turn onto a floured surface and knead lightly until smooth. Wrap in cling wrap and refrigerate for 30 minutes.
3 To make filling, place pumpkin, eggs, sour cream, cream, golden syrup, nutmeg, mixed spice and cinnamon in a mixing bowl and beat until smooth and well combined.
4 Roll pastry out and line a buttered 9 in/23cm flan tin with removable base. Spoon filling into pastry case. Bake for 20 minutes, then reduce heat to 320°F/160° and bake for 25–30 minutes longer or until filling is set and pastry golden. Allow to stand in tin for 5 minutes before removing. Serve hot, warm or cold with whipped cream.

Serves 8 • Preparation 45 minutes • Cooking 50 minutes

Fresh fruit tartlets

Sweet almond pastry
¼ cup plain flour
¾ cups self-raising flour
⅓ cup cornflour
⅓ cup ground almonds
¼ cup icing sugar
5 oz/150g butter
1 egg yolk

Filling
3½ oz/100g ricotta cheese
¼ cup sugar
3½ oz/100g pure cream
¼ cup milk mixed with 1 tablespoon of arrowroot
½ cup cooked white short-grain rice or semolina
fruit for decorating (for example, blueberries, strawberries, peaches, mangoes, kiwifruit)
¼ cup apple and blackcurrant baby jelly, warmed

1 Preheat oven to 380°F/190°C. To make the pastry, combine flours, almonds and sugar in a bowl. Rub in butter until mixture resembles fine breadcrumbs. Stir in egg and enough iced water (about ¼ cup) to make ingredients just come together. Knead on a floured surface until smooth. Wrap in cling wrap. Refrigerate for at least 30 minutes.

2 Roll out pastry to ⅛ in/3mm thick. Using a 3 in/75mm round fluted cutter, cut out 24 rounds. Gently ease pastry into buttered muffin or patty pans. Prick all over with a fork. Line with foil or baking paper. Weigh down with uncooked rice and bake for 10 minutes. Remove rice and foil. Bake for a further 5–6 minutes or until golden, then cool.

3 Mix ricotta cheese, sugar and cream until light and smooth. Combine ricotta mixture and milk mixture in a saucepan. Cook, stirring, over medium heat for 5–10 minutes or until mixture starts to thicken. Cool. Divide mixture between pastry cases. Top with fruit. Brush with warmed jelly. Chill until ready to serve.

Makes 24 • Preparation 50 minutes • Cooking 25 minutes

Fruit mince pies

Fruit filling
¼ cup mixed peel
¼ cup sultanas
¼ cup raisins
¼ cup currants
¼ cup chopped dried apricots
¼ cup drained, canned crushed
  unsweetened pineapple
1 apple, finely chopped
2 tablespoons finely chopped almonds or
  hazelnuts
1 teaspoon grated lemon zest
1 teaspoon grated orange zest
1 tablespoon orange juice

2 tablespoons brown sugar
1 teaspoon ground cloves
1 teaspoon ground cinnamon
1 teaspoon mixed spice
1 tablespoon rum

Sweet almond pastry
¼ cup plain flour
¾ cups self-raising flour
⅓ cup cornflour
⅓ cup ground almonds
¼ cup icing sugar
5 oz/150g butter
1 egg yolk

1 To prepare the filling, place all ingredients in a bowl. Mix well. Place in an airtight container. Refrigerate for at least 5 days, turning occasionally.

2 To make the pastry, combine flours, almonds and sugar in a bowl. Rub in butter until mixture resembles fine breadcrumbs. Stir in egg and enough iced water (about ¼ cup) to make ingredients just come together. Knead on a floured surface until smooth. Wrap in cling wrap. Refrigerate for at least 30 minutes.

3 Preheat oven to 360°F/180°C.

4 Roll out pastry to ⅛ in/3mm thick. Cut pastry into 24 rounds, using a 3 in/75mm cutter. Cut remaining pastry into decorative shapes or rounds for top of pies.

5 Gently ease pastry rounds into buttered patty or muffin pans. Divide filling between pastry cases. Top with decorative pastry shapes. Brush pastry with egg white. Bake for 20–25 minutes or until golden.

Makes 24 • Preparation 30 minutes, plus standing time • Cooking 25 minutes

Cornish pasties

1 egg, lightly beaten

Pastry
2 oz/60g butter, softened
2 oz/60g lard, softened
2 cups plain flour, sifted

Beef and vegetable filling
8 oz/250g lean beef mince
1 small onion, grated
1 potato, peeled and grated
½ small turnip, peeled and grated
¼ cup fresh parsley, chopped
1 tablespoon Worcestershire sauce
freshly ground black pepper

1 Preheat oven to 440°F/220°C.

2 To make pastry, place butter and lard in a bowl and mix well to combine. Cover and refrigerate until firm. Place flour in a bowl. Chop butter mixture into small pieces and, using fingertips, rub into flour until mixture resembles coarse breadcrumbs. Mix in enough cold water (about ⅓ cup) to form a soft dough, then turn pastry onto a floured surface and knead lightly. Wrap in cling wrap and chill for 30 minutes.

3 To make filling, place meat, onion, potato, turnip, parsley, Worcestershire sauce and black pepper to taste in a bowl and mix well to combine.

4 Roll out pastry on a lightly floured surface to ¼ in/6mm thick and, using an upturned saucer as a guide, cut out six 6 in/15cm rounds. Divide filling between pastry rounds. Brush edges with water and fold the pastry rounds in half upwards to enclose filling.

5 Press pastry edges together to seal, then flute between finger and thumb. Place pasties on a buttered baking tray, brush with egg and bake for 15 minutes. Reduce oven temperature to 320°F/160°C and bake for 20 minutes or until golden.

Makes 6 • Preparation 45 minutes • Cooking 35 minutes

Individual meat pies

1½ lb/750g prepared shortcrust pastry
13 oz/375g prepared puff pastry
1 egg, lightly beaten

Beef filling
1½ lb/750g lean beef mince
2 cups beef stock
freshly ground black pepper
2 tablespoons cornflour, blended with ½ cup water
1 tablespoon Worcestershire sauce
1 teaspoon soy sauce

1 Preheat oven to 440°F/220°C.
2 To make filling, heat a frying pan over a medium heat, add meat and cook until brown. Drain off juices, stir in stock and black pepper to taste and bring to the boil. Reduce heat, cover and simmer for 20 minutes. Stir in cornflour mixture and Worcestershire and soy sauces and cook, stirring, until mixture boils and thickens. Cool.
3 Roll out shortcrust pastry to ⅕ in/5mm thick and use to line base and sides of eight buttered, small metal pie dishes. Roll out puff pastry to ⅕ in/5mm thick and cut out rounds to fit top of pies.
4 Divide filling between pie dishes. Brush edges of shortcrust pastry with water, top with rounds of puff pastry and press edges together to seal. Brush pies with egg and bake for 5 minutes, then reduce oven temperature to 360°F/180°C and bake for a further 10–15 minutes or until pastry is golden.

Makes 8 • Preparation 25 minutes • Cooking 45 minutes

Beef and mushroom pie

Puff Pastry
30 oz/90g butter, softened
30 oz/90g lard, softened
2 cups plain flour

Beef and mushroom filling
2 lb/1kg lean beef, cut into
  1 in/25mm cubes
¼ cup seasoned plain flour

30 oz/90g butter
3 tablespoons olive oil
2 onions, chopped
2 cloves garlic, crushed
2 cups button mushrooms,
  sliced
½ cup red wine
½ cup beef stock

1 bay leaf
¼ cup fresh parsley, finely
  chopped
1 tablespoon
  Worcestershire sauce
freshly ground black
  pepper
1 egg, lightly beaten

1 For the filling, toss meat in flour to coat. Shake off excess. Melt butter and oil in
  a large heavy-based saucepan and cook meat in batches for 3–4 minutes, or until
  browned. Remove meat from pan and set aside.

2 Add onions and garlic to pan and cook over medium heat for 3–4 minutes, or until
  softened. Stir in mushrooms and cook for 2 minutes longer. Combine the wine and
  stock, pour into pan and cook for 4–5 minutes. Bring to the boil, then reduce heat.
  Return meat to the pan with bay leaf, parsley, Worcestershire sauce and pepper to
  taste. Cover and simmer for 1½ hours or until the meat is tender. Remove pan from
  the heat and set aside to cool.

3 For the pastry, mix butter and lard until well combined. Cover and refrigerate until
  firm. Place flour in a large mixing bowl. Cut butter mixture into small pieces and rub
  a quater into flour with your fingertips until mixture resembles bread crumbs. Add
  enough cold water to form a firm dough (about ½ cup).

4 Turn pastry onto a floured surface and knead lightly. Roll to a 6 x 10 in/15 x 25cm
  rectangle. Place another quarter of butter mixture over top two-thirds of pastry. Fold
  bottom third of pastry up and top a third down to give 3 even layers. Half turn to have
  the open end facing you, and roll to a rectangle as before. Repeat the folding and rolling
  twice, adding more butter mixture each time. Cover pastry and refrigerate 1 hour.

5 Preheat oven to 380°F/190°C. Place cooled filling in a 4-cup capacity pie dish. Roll
  out pastry 1 in/25mm larger than the pie dish. Cut off a ½ in/12mm strip from pastry
  edge. Brush the pastry strip with water. Lift the pastry top over the filling and press
  gently to seal the edges. Trim and knock back edges. Brush with egg and bake for
  30 minutes or until the pastry is golden and crisp.

Serves 4 • Preparation 1 hour 30 minutes • Cooking 2 hours

Old English pork pie

1 egg yolk, lightly beaten with
  1 tablespoon water

Hot water pastry
2 cups flour, sifted
1 teaspoon salt
4 oz/125g lard

Pork filling
3 lb/1½kg lean boneless pork, cut into
  small cubes
½ teaspoon ground sage
freshly ground black pepper
2 cups chicken consommé

1 Preheat oven to 480°F/250°C. To make pastry, combine flour and salt in a bowl and make a well in the centre.

2 Place lard and ⅔ cup water in a saucepan and heat over a medium heat until lard melts and mixture comes to the boil. Pour boiling liquid into flour and mix to form a firm dough. Turn pastry onto a floured surface and knead lightly until smooth. Cover and stand for 10 minutes.

3 Lightly knead two-thirds of the pastry on a lightly floured surface, then roll out to 5mm thick and use to line the base and sides of a buttered, deep 8 in/20cm springform tin. Bake for 15 minutes, then set aside to cool.

4 To make filling, place pork, sage and black pepper to taste in a bowl and mix to combine. Pack filling firmly into pastry case and brush edges with a little of the egg yolk mixture.

5 Knead remaining pastry, then roll out to a ⅛ in/5mm thick circle, large enough to cover pie. Cut a 1 in/25mm circle from centre of pastry top. Place pastry over filling, trim and press top to pastry case. Brush top with remaining egg yolk mixture and bake for 30 minutes. Reduce oven temperature to 320°F/160°C and bake for 1½ hours. Using a spoon, remove any juices that appear in the hole during cooking. Remove from oven and cool in tin for 2 hours.

6 Heat consommé in a saucepan over low heat and cook until it melts. Cool slightly, then gradually pour into pie through hole in the top. Cool, then refrigerate pie overnight.

Serves 8 • Preparation 40 minutes, plus standing time • Cooking 2 hours

Potato, egg and leek pies

1 lb/500g shortcrust pastry
1 egg, lightly beaten

Potato and leek filling
1 oz/30g butter
4 leeks, sliced
2 cloves garlic, crushed
2 teaspoons curry powder
6 potatoes, cooked until tender, chopped
10½ oz/300g asparagus, stalks removed, chopped and blanched
4 hard boiled eggs, chopped
4 oz/125g aged Cheddar cheese, grated
¼ cup fresh parsley, chopped
⅔ cup sour cream
2 egg yolks, lightly beaten
freshly ground black pepper
1 egg, lightly beaten
caraway seeds

1 Preheat ovent to 440°F/220°C.

2 To make filling, melt butter in a frying pan over a low heat, add leeks and cook for 3–4 minutes or until soft. Increase heat to medium, stir in garlic and curry powder and cook for 1 minute. Combine potatoes, leek mixture, asparagus, chopped eggs, cheese, parsley, sour cream, egg yolks and black pepper to taste. Cool completely.

3 Roll out shortcrust pastry to ⅕ in/5mm thick cut to fit the base and sides of ten buttered, metal pie dishes. Cut remaining pastry to fit top of pies. Spoon filling into pie dishes, brush pastry edges with egg and top with pie lids. Press pastry edges together to seal. Using a sharp knife, make a slit on the top of each pie, then brush with egg and bake for 15 minutes. Reduce oven temperature to 360°F/180°C and bake for 15 minutes or until golden.

Makes 10 pies • Preparation 25 minutes • Cooking 40 minutes

desserts

It is curious that no matter how satisfied we are after a meal, our tastebuds tell us there is always room for something sweet. Our 'dessert' stomach becomes surprisingly barren in the face of creamy puddings, floaty soufflés, the textured cherry-flavoured clafouti, the buttery goodness of a crumble or the crispy soft-filled meringue of pavlova.

The perfect pavlova

6 egg whites
1½ cups caster sugar
6 teaspoons cornflour, sifted
1½ teaspoons white vinegar
11 oz/315mL thickened cream, whipped
selection of fresh fruits, such as orange segments, sliced bananas, sliced peaches,
 passionfruit pulp, berries or sliced kiwifruit

1 Preheat oven to 240°F/120°C.
2 Place egg whites in a mixing bowl and beat until soft peaks form. Gradually add
   sugar, beating well after each addition, until mixture is thick and glossy.
3 Fold cornflour and vinegar into egg white mixture. Butter a baking tray and line with
   non-stick baking paper. Butter paper and dust lightly with flour. Mark a 9 in/23cm
   diameter circle on paper.
4 Place the egg white mixture in the centre of the circle and spread out to within edge
   of circle and neaten using a metal spatula or knife. Bake for 1½–2 hours or until firm
   to touch. Turn off oven and cool pavlova in oven with door ajar. Decorate cold pavlova
   with cream and top with fruit.

Serves 8 • Preparation 25 minutes • Cooking 2 hours

Rhubarb soufflé

1 lb/500g rhubarb, trimmed and cut into 1 in/25mm pieces
½ cup sugar
4 teaspoons cornflour, blended with ¼ cup water
½ cup caster sugar
5 egg whites
icing sugar, sifted

1 Preheat ovent to 440°F/220°C.
2 Place rhubarb, ½ cup water and the sugar in a saucepan and cook over a medium heat for 10 minutes or until rhubarb softens.
3 Stir in cornflour mixture and cook for 2–3 minutes longer or until mixture thickens. Set aside to cool slightly.
4 Place egg whites in a large mixing bowl and beat until soft peaks form. Gradually add caster sugar, beating well after each addition, until mixture is thick and glossy. Fold in rhubarb mixture and spoon into a buttered 8 in/20cm soufflé dish. Bake for 15–20 minutes or until soufflé is well risen and golden brown. Dust with icing sugar and serve immediately.

Serves 8 • Preparation 20 minutes • Cooking 40 minutes

Brandied plum clafouti

1 lb/500g plums, quartered and stoned
⅓ cup brandy
2 tablespoons sugar
¼ cup plain flour, sifted
¼ cup caster sugar
3 eggs, lightly beaten
1 cup milk
1 teaspoon vanilla extract

Brandy orange sauce
¾ cup orange juice
2 tablespoons sugar
½ teaspoon ground cinnamon
2 teaspoons arrowroot, blended with 4 teaspoons water

1 Preheat oven to 360°F/180°C.
2 Place plums and brandy in a bowl, sprinkle with sugar, cover and set aside to stand
   for 30 minutes. Drain plums and reserve liquid. Arrange plums in a lightly buttered
   ovenproof dish.
3 Place flour and caster sugar in a bowl, add eggs, milk and vanilla extract and stir until
   batter is smooth. Pour batter evenly over plums. Bake for 45–50 minutes or until firm.
4 To make sauce, place reserved brandy liquid, orange juice, sugar, cinnamon and
   arrowroot mixture in a small saucepan and cook over a medium heat, stirring
   constantly, until mixture boils and thickens. Accompany clafouti with brandy orange
   sauce and whipped cream, if desired.

Serves 4 • Preparation 50 minutes • Cooking 50 minutes

Apple and berry crumble

¼ cup caster sugar
4 green apples, peeled, cored and sliced
15 oz/440g canned blueberries, drained

Crumble topping
1¾ cups crushed shortbread biscuits
1½ oz/45g unsalted butter, softened
4 tablespoons ground almonds
2 tablespoons demerara sugar
½ teaspoon ground cinnamon
1 egg yolk
1½ tablespoons double cream

1 Preheat oven to 360°F/180°C.
2 Place sugar and ½ cup water in a saucepan and cook over a medium heat, stirring constantly, until sugar dissolves. Bring to the boil, then add apples and cook, over a low heat, for 8–10 minutes or until apples are tender. Remove from heat and set aside to cool.
3 Drain apples and combine with blueberries. Spoon apple mixture into a buttered, shallow ovenproof dish.
4 To make topping, place crushed biscuits, butter, almonds, sugar, cinnamon, egg yolk and cream in a mixing bowl and mix until just combined. Sprinkle topping over apple mixture and bake for 20–25 minutes or until golden.

Serves 6 • Preparation 30 minutes • Cooking 40 minutes

Sweet pumpkin coyotas

Coyotas dough
20 oz/625g plain flour
10 oz/300g butter, chopped
pinch of salt

Sweet pumpkin filling
1½ lb/750g butternut pumpkin, peeled and chopped
½ cup brown sugar
1½ oz/45g butter, diced

1 Preheat oven to 400°F/200°C.
2 To make filling, place pumpkin in a baking dish, then scatter with sugar, dot with butter and drizzle with water. Cover and bake for 30–40 minutes or until pumpkin is soft and golden. Cool.
3 To make dough, place flour, butter and salt in a food processor and process until mixture resembles fine breadcrumbs. With machine running, add enough cold water to form a soft dough, about ¾ cup. Turn dough onto a lightly floured surface and knead for 10 minutes or until soft and elastic. Chill.
4 Divide dough into 16 equal pieces. Roll out each piece to form a ⅛ in/3mm thick round.
5 Place 1–2 tablespoons of filling in the centre of 8 of the dough rounds. Top with remaining rounds and press edges to seal. Place coyotas on buttered baking trays, reduce oven temperature to 360°F/180°C and bake for 25–30 minutes or until golden. Serve warm.

Makes 8 • Preparation 20 minutes • Cooking 1 hour 20 minutes

Apple and rhubarb crumble

8 stalks rhubarb, cut into 2 in/5cm pieces
4 cooking apples, cored, peeled and sliced
½ cup caster sugar
¼ cup orange juice

Hazelnut crumble
½ cup ground hazelnuts
½ cup rolled oats
⅓ cup plain flour
¼ cup brown sugar
3 tablespoons desiccated coconut
¼ teaspoon ground cinnamon
3 oz/90g butter, chopped into small pieces

1 Preheat oven to 360°F/180°C.
2 Place rhubarb, apples, caster sugar, ½ cup water and the orange juice in a saucepan and cook, stirring constantly, over a medium heat, until sugar dissolves. Bring to the boil, then reduce heat, cover and simmer for 10 minutes or until fruit is tender. Spoon fruit mixture into a 3-cup capacity ovenproof dish.
3 To make crumble, place hazelnuts, oats, flour, brown sugar, coconut and cinnamon in a bowl and mix to combine. Using fingertips, rub in butter until mixture resembles coarse breadcrumbs. Sprinkle crumble over fruit mixture and bake for 20–25 minutes.

Serves 4 • Preparation 20 minutes • Cooking 35 minutes

Pear upside down pudding

¼ cup demerara sugar
2 x 15 oz/440g canned pear halves, drained and 1 cup syrup reserved
8 oz/250g butter, softened
2 cups self-raising flour
1 cup caster sugar
4 eggs
1 cup chopped walnuts
¼ cup maple syrup

1 Preheat oven to 360°F/180°C.

2 Sprinkle base of a buttered and lined, deep 9 in/23cm round cake tin with demerara sugar. Cut pear halves in half to form quarters and arrange cut-side up, over base.

3 Place butter, flour, sugar and eggs in a food processor and process until smooth. Stir in walnuts. Carefully spoon batter over fruit in tin and bake for 1–1¼ hours or until cooked when tested with a skewer.

4 Place maple syrup and reserved pear juice in a saucepan over a medium heat and cook until syrup is reduced by half.

5 Turn pudding onto a serving plate and pour over syrup. Serve with cream or ice cream.

Serves 8 • Preparation 20 minutes • Cooking 1 hour 15 minutes

Citrus delicious pudding

1 cup caster sugar
4 oz/125g butter, softened
½ cup self-raising flour
1 tablespoon finely grated lemon zest
1 tablespoon finely grated orange zest
2 tablespoons lemon juice
2 tablespoons orange juice
2 eggs, separated
1 cup milk

1 Preheat oven to 360°F/180°C.
2 Place sugar and butter in a bowl and beat until light and fluffy. Stir in flour, lemon and orange zests and lemon and orange juices.
3 Place egg yolks and milk in a bowl and whisk to combine. Stir into citrus mixture.
4 Place egg whites in a bowl and beat until stiff peaks form, then fold into batter. Spoon batter into a buttered 4-cup capacity ovenproof dish. Place dish in a baking pan with enough boiling water to come halfway up the sides of dish. Bake for 45 minutes or until cooked.

Serves 6 • Preparation 20 minutes • Cooking 45 minutes

Baked fresh dates and apples

5 large cooking apples
7 oz/200g fresh dates, stoned and halved
juice of ½ lemon
juice of 2 oranges
zest of 1 orange, finely grated
2 cinnamon sticks
3 tablespoons clear honey

1 Preheat oven to 360°F/180°C.
2 Peel and thinly slice the apples. Place in a shallow buttered oven-proof dish. Stir in the dates, juices, zest and cinnamon sticks. Drizzle the honey over the mixture.
3 Cover and bake for 45–55 minutes (until tender and flavours are absorbed).
4 Serve warm or chilled with Greek yoghurt, dusted with cinnamon.

Serves 4 • Preparation 25 minutes • Cooking 55 minutes

Grand Marnier soufflé

½ cup orange juice
1 teaspoon grated orange zest
¾ cup cooked long-grain rice
4 egg yolks
1 tablespoon caster sugar, plus ⅓ cup
1 tablespoon cornflour
1¼ cups milk
4 tablespoons Grand Marnier
5 egg whites

1 Preheat oven to 440°F/220°C.
2 Place orange juice, zest and rice in a saucepan and bring to the boil. Reduce heat and allow to simmer, stirring occasionally until all liquid has been absorbed. Set aside.
3 Whisk together egg yolks, 1 tablespoon caster sugar and cornflour. Heat milk in a saucepan until just at boiling point. Add to egg yolk mixture, whisk, then return mixture to saucepan. Stir over medium heat until custard boils and thickens. Reduce heat and simmer for 3–4 minutes, stirring constantly. Remove from heat. Stir in Grand Marnier and rice mixture. Cool slightly.
4 Beat egg whites until stiff peaks form. Add extra sugar, a tablespoon at a time, beating after each addition. Stir a little beaten egg white into rice custard then lightly fold in remaining whites. Spoon into prepared soufflé dish. Bake for 20–25 minutes until soufflé is puffed and golden. Serve immediately.

Serves 4 • Preparation 30 minutes • Cooking 40 minutes

cakes

Commemorating birthdays, weddings, anniversaries – virtually any celebration – or for no reason at all, life would not be complete without the humble cake. A baked confection of flour, sugar, eggs, and butter or oil, cakes may be simply dusted in icing sugar or elaborately frosted with multiple layers of fresh or butter-cream, jams, curds or frosting and embellished with piped borders.

Raspberry chocolate truffle cakes

½ cup cocoa powder, sifted
4 oz/125g butter
1¾ cups caster sugar
2 eggs
1⅔ cups self-raising flour, sifted
14 oz/400g dark chocolate, melted
fresh raspberries

Raspberry cream
4 oz/125g raspberries, puréed and sieved
½ cup thickened cream, whipped

1 Preheat oven to 360°F/180°C.

2 Combine cocoa powder and 1 cup boiling water. Mix to dissolve and set aside to cool.

3 Place butter and sugar in a bowl and beat until light and fluffy. Beat in eggs, one at a time, adding a little flour with each egg. Fold remaining flour and cocoa mixture, alternately, into creamed butter mixture.

4 Spoon mixture into eight lightly buttered ½-cup capacity ramekins or large muffin tins. Bake for 20–25 minutes or until cakes are cooked when tested with a skewer. Cool for 5 minutes, then turn onto wire racks to cool. Turn cakes upside down and scoop out centre, leaving a ½ in/12mm shell. Spread each cake with chocolate to cover top and sides, then place right way up on a wire rack.

5 To make cream, fold raspberry purée into cream. Spoon cream into a piping bag fitted with a large nozzle. Carefully turn cakes upside down and pipe in cream to fill cavity. Place right way up on individual serving plates. Garnish with fresh raspberries.

Serves 8 • Preparation 25 minutes • Cooking 25 minutes

Spiced apple cake

2 apples, cored, peeled and sliced
4 oz/125g butter
1 cup raw or demerara sugar
2 eggs
1 cup self-raising flour
1 cup wholemeal flour
½ teaspoon baking soda
1½ teaspoons ground mixed spice
1 oz/30g walnuts, chopped
2 oz/60g raisins, chopped
¾ cup thickened cream, whipped
icing sugar, sifted

1 Preheat oven to 360°F/180°C.

2 Place apples and ¾ cup water in a saucepan and cook over a medium heat until tender. Place in a food processor or blender and process until smooth. Set aside to cool.

3 Place butter and sugar in a bowl and beat until light and fluffy. Add eggs, one at a time, beating well after each addition.

4 Sift together self-raising flour, wholemeal flour, baking soda and 1 teaspoon of the mixed spice into a bowl. Return husks to bowl. Mix flour mixture and apple mixture, alternately, into butter mixture, then stir in walnuts and raisins.

5 Spoon batter into a buttered and lined 9 in/23cm round cake tin and bake for 40 minutes or until cooked when tested with a skewer. Allow to cool in tin for 5 minutes before turning onto a wire rack to cool completely.

6 Split cake in half horizontally, spread bottom half with cream, then top with other half and dust with remaining mixed spice and icing sugar.

Makes one cake • Preparation 20 minutes • Cooking 50 minutes

Orange poppy seed cake

4 tablespoons poppy seeds
¼ cup orange juice
4 oz/125g natural yoghurt
7 oz/200g butter, softened
1 tablespoon finely grated orange zest
1 cup caster sugar
3 eggs
2 cups self-raising flour, sifted
2 tablespoons orange marmalade, warmed

1 Preheat oven to 360°F/180°C.
2 Place poppy seeds, orange juice and yoghurt into a bowl, mix to combine and set aside to stand for 1 hour.
3 Place butter and orange zest in a bowl and beat until light and fluffy. Gradually add sugar, beating well after each addition until mixture is creamy.
4 Add eggs one at a time, beating well after each addition. Fold flour and poppy seed mixture, alternately, into butter mixture.
5 Spoon batter into a buttered 8 in/20cm fluted ring tin and bake for 35–40 minutes or until cooked when tested with a skewer. Stand in tin for 5 minutes before turning onto a wire rack to cool completely. Brush with orange marmalade before serving.

Makes one cake • Preparation 1 hour 20 minutes • Cooking 40 minutes

Pecan and almond cakes

2 eggs, separated
½ cup caster sugar
few drops of vanilla extract
½ cup plain flour
1 teaspoon baking powder
¼ cup mixed pecans and almonds, chopped
2 tablespoons icing sugar

1 Preheat oven to 300°F/150°C.
2 Butter 12 individual bun tins. Whisk egg yolks with sugar until thick and pale.
   Gently stir in vanilla. Sift together flour and baking powder over surface of egg
   yolk mixture, then fold in.
3 In a clean bowl, whisk egg whites until stiff then fold gently into egg yolk mixture.
   Carefully fold nuts into mixture. Divide among prepared bun tins and bake for
   15 minutes. Sieve icing sugar over and serve warm..

Makes 12 • Preparation 20 minutes • Cooking 15 minutes

Victoria sandwich cake

4 eggs
¾ cup caster sugar
1 cup self-raising flour
1 tablespoon cornflour
1½ teaspoons melted butter
1 tablespoon icing sugar, sifted

Jam and cream filling
½ cup strawberry jam
½ cup thickened cream, whipped

1 Preheat oven to 360°F/180°C.
2 Place eggs in a bowl and beat until thick and creamy. Gradually beat in caster sugar and continue beating until mixture becomes thick. This will take about 10 minutes.
3 Sift flour and cornflour together over egg mixture, then fold in. Stir in ⅓ cup warm water and the melted butter.
4 Divide mixture evenly between two buttered and lined 8 in/20cm round sandwich tins.
5 Bake for 20–25 minutes or until cakes shrink slightly from sides of tins and spring back when touched with the fingertips. Stand cakes in tins for 5 minutes before turning onto wire racks to cool.
6 To assemble, spread one cake with jam, then top with whipped cream and remaining sponge cake. Just prior to serving, dust cake with icing sugar.

Makes one cake • Preparation 30 minutes • Cooking 25 minutes

cheesecakes

When presented with a delicious cake menu, some connoisseurs will search through pages of sumptuous baked goodies for the only kind that will hit the spot: cheesecake. For some cake-lovers, there can be no substitute for that special combination of a crumbly biscuit crust and a cream-cheese filling. With the addition of chocolate, toffee, nuts, fruit – even bourbon! – there is a favourite cheesecake for everybody.

Orange and lime cheesecake

1 cup plain sweet biscuits, crushed
2 oz/60g butter, melted
shredded coconut, toasted

Orange and lime filling
9 oz/250g cream cheese, softened
2 tablespoons brown sugar
1½ teaspoons finely grated orange zest
1½ teaspoons finely grated lime zest
3 teaspoons orange juice
3 teaspoons lime juice
1 egg, lightly beaten
½ cup sweetened condensed milk
2 tablespoons double cream, whipped

1 Preheat oven to 360°F/180°C.
2 Place the biscuits and butter in a bowl and mix to combine. Press the biscuit mixture over the base and up the sides of a well-buttered 9 in/23cm flan tin with a removable base. Bake for 5–8 minutes, then cool.
3 To make the orange and lime filling, place the cream cheese, sugar, orange and lime zests and juices in a bowl and beat until creamy. Beat in the egg, then mix in the condensed milk and fold in the cream.
4 Spoon the filling into the prepared biscuit case and bake for 25–30 minutes or until just firm. Turn the oven off and cool the cheesecake in the oven with the door ajar. Chill before serving. Serve decorated with the toasted coconut.

Serves 8 • Preparation 30 minutes • Cooking 40 minutes

Almond cheesecake

¾ cup caster sugar
2 oz/60g butter, softened
1 lb/500g cream cheese
¼ cup plain flour, sifted
2 tablespoons honey
5 eggs, separated
½ cup double cream
1 teaspoon vanilla extract
2½ oz/75g blanched almonds, finely chopped

Brown sugar topping
¼ cup brown sugar
3 tablespoons finely chopped blanched almonds
1 teaspoon ground cinnamon

1 Preheat oven to 300°F/150°C.
2 To make topping, place brown sugar, almonds and cinnamon in a bowl and mix to combine. Set aside.
3 Place caster sugar and butter in a bowl and beat until light and fluffy. Beat in cream cheese and continue beating until mixture is creamy. Beat in flour, honey and egg yolks and continue beating until well combined. Fold in cream and vanilla extract. Place egg whites in a bowl and beat until stiff peaks form. Fold egg whites and almonds into cream cheese mixture.
4 Spoon mixture into a buttered and lined 10 in/25cm springform tin. Sprinkle with topping and bake for 1½ hours or until just firm. Turn off oven and leave cheesecake in oven to cool.

Serves 8 • Preparation 30 minutes • Cooking 1 hour 30 minutes

Chocolate caramel cheesecake

Base
5½ oz/150g digestive biscuits, finely crushed
2 oz/60g butter, melted

Filling
¼ cup evaporated milk
14 oz/400g canned caramel
1 cup pecans, chopped
1 lb/500g cream cheese
½ cup sugar
2 eggs
1 teaspoon vanilla extract
¾ cup chocolate chips, melted

1 Preheat oven to 360°F/180°C.

2 To make the base, combine crumbs and melted butter. Press mixture evenly into a 9 in/23cm springform tin. Bake for 8 minutes. Remove from oven and allow to cool.

3 To make the filling, combine milk and caramel in a heavy-based saucepan. Cook over low heat until melted, stirring often. Pour over biscuit base. Sprinkle pecans evenly over caramel layer and set aside.

4 Beat cream cheese at high speed with electric mixer until light and fluffy. Gradually add sugar, mixing well. Add eggs one at a time, beating well after each addition. Stir in vanilla and melted chocolate, beat until blended. Pour over pecan layer.

5 Bake for 30 minutes. Remove from oven and run knife around edge of tin to release sides. Cool to room temperature. Cover and chill for 8 hours.

6 Decorate with a chopped flaky chocolate bar and chopped jersey caramels. Serve with whipped cream.

Makes 12 slices • Preparation 30 minutes, plus standing time • Cooking 40 minutes

Sultana and bourbon cheesecake

Base
2 oz/60g digestive biscuits, finely crushed
1 oz/30g butter, melted
¼ cup sugar

Filling
1½ cups raisins
¼ cup Bourbon
1 lb/500g cream cheese, softened
¼ cup sugar
1 tablespoon lemon juice
zest of ½ lemon
2 large eggs

1 Preheat oven to 330°F/165°C.

2 Soak the raisins in the Bourbon for at least 2 hours.

3 To make the base, combine crumbs, butter and sugar. Line four 4 in/10cm springform tins with baking paper, then press mixture evenly onto bottoms of tins. Bake for 5 minutes.

4 To make the filling, combine cream cheese, sugar, juice and zest in an electric mixer, mix on medium speed until well blended. Add eggs one at a time, mixing thoroughly between additions. Chop 1 cup of the soaked raisins roughly and add to the filling, then divide filling evenly between tins.

5 Bake for 25 minutes. Cool before removing from tins, then chill.

6 Let stand at room temperature for minimum of 40 minutes. Decorate with the remaining raisins and serve with whipped cream.

Serves 4 • Preparation 30 minutes, plus standing time • Cooking 30 minutes

Hazelnut raspberry cheesecake

7 oz/200g ameretti biscuits, finely crushed
2 oz/60g butter, melted

Filling
2 lb/1kg cream cheese, softened
1¼ cups sugar
3 large eggs
1 cup sour cream
1 teaspoon vanilla extract
6 oz/170g hazelnut spread
⅓ cup raspberry conserve

1 Preheat oven to 330°F/165°C.

2 To make the base, combine crumbs and butter, press onto bottom of a 9 in/23cm springform tin.

3 To make the filling, combine three-quarters of the cream cheese with the sugar in an electric mixer and mix on medium speed until well blended. Add eggs one at a time, beating well after each addition. Blend in sour cream and vanilla, then pour over base.

4 Combine remaining cream cheese and the hazelnut spread in the electric mixer, mix on medium speed until well blended. Add raspberry conserve, mix well.

5 Drop heaped tablespoonfuls of hazelnut mixture into plain cream cheese filling – do not swirl.

6 Bake for 1 hour and 25 minutes. Loosen cake from rim of tin, cool before removing. Serve with fresh raspberries.

Makes 12 slices • Preparation 30 minutes • Cooking 1 hour 25 minutes

Mini passionfruit cheesecake

Base
2 oz/60g digestive biscuits, finely crushed
1 oz/30g butter, melted
¼ cup sugar

Filling
1 lb/500g cream cheese, softened
¼ cup passionfruit pulp, strained
1 teaspoon vanilla extract
¼ cup sugar
2 large eggs
4 fresh passionfruit

1 Preheat oven to 330°F/165°C.
2 To make the base, combine crumbs, butter and sugar. Line four 4 in/10cm springform tins with baking paper, then press mixture evenly onto bottoms of tins. Bake for 5 minutes.
3 To make the filling, combine cream cheese, passionfruit pulp, vanilla and sugar in an electric mixer, mix on medium speed until well combined. Add the eggs one at a time, mixing well after each addition. Divide filling evenly between the bases.
4 Bake for 25 minutes. Cool before removing from tins.
5 Decorate with fresh passionfruit and serve.

Serves 4 • Preparation 30 minutes • Cooking 30 minutes

Papaya lime cheesecake

Base
¼ cup sugar
1 oz/30g butter, softened
11½ oz/330g gingernut biscuits, finely
  crushed

Filling
6 oz/180g cottage cheese
9 oz/250g cream cheese, softened
1 cup sour cream
½ cup sugar

½ cup coconut cream
¼ cup plain flour
1 teaspoon coconut extract
3 eggs

Topping
1½ cups caster sugar
3–4 fresh limes, thinly sliced
¼ papaya, cubed

1 Preheat oven to 350°F/175°C.

2 To make the base, mix together the sugar, butter and biscuit crumbs in a bowl. Press into a lined 9 in/23cm springform tin.

3 Bake for 12 minutes, cool on a wire rack. Lower heat to 300°F/150°C.

4 To make the filling, place cheeses in a food processor, process for 2 minutes or until smooth, scraping sides of processor bowl once. Add sour cream, sugar, coconut cream, flour, coconut extract and eggs, process for 20 seconds, scraping sides of processor bowl once.

5 Pour cheese mixture into base, bake for 1½ hours or until almost set. Turn oven off, and let cheesecake stand for 1 hour in oven with door closed. Remove cheesecake from oven, cover and chill for 1 hour.

6 To make the topping, place 1 cup water and 1 cup of sugar in a pan. Bring to the boil and simmer until sugar dissolves. Add the lime slices and simmer for 10 minutes. Meanwhile, place the remaining sugar on a tray.

7 Remove the lime slices from the heat, strain and dry on absorbent paper. Cool slightly, then place one at a time on the tray of sugar to coat. Decorate the cheesecake with the lime slices and papaya.

Makes 12 slices • Preparation 40 minutes, plus standing time • Cooking 1 hour 45 minutes

Ginger honey cheesecake

Base
8 oz/250g gingernut biscuits, finely crushed
1 tablespoon sugar
2 oz/60g butter, chilled

Filling
1 lb/500g cream cheese, softened
½ cup honey
½ cup sugar
2 large eggs, at room temperature
10 oz/300g kashta cheese
1 tablespoon lemon juice
1½ teaspoons vanilla extract
¾ cup dates, finely minced
2 tablespoons glacé ginger, finely minced

1 Preheat oven to 360°F/180°C.

2 To make the base, butter only the sides of a 9 in/23cm springform tin. Mix the crumbs and sugar in a bowl. Add the butter and rub it in well with your fingers. Distribute the crumbs loosely but evenly in the pan and push them slightly up the sides. Cover and chill while you make the filling.

3 To make the filling, using an electric mixer, cream the cream cheese, honey and sugar until light and fluffy. Beat in the eggs one at a time, then add the remaining ingredients and continue to beat until evenly blended. Pour the filling into the tin and bake for 1 hour and 15 minutes. Cool thoroughly on a rack, then cover, still in the tin, and refrigerate for 12 hours before removing from the tin and slicing.

4 Dust the cheesecake with icing sugar before serving.

Makes 12 slices • Preparation 20 minutes, plus standing time • Cooking 1 hour 15 minutes

Toffee cheesecake

Base
3½ oz/100g vanilla wafers, finely crushed
3 oz/90g butter, melted

Filling
14 oz/400g caramel sweets
1 cup semi-sweet chocolate chips
½ cup evaporated milk
3 chocolate bars covered in toffee,
  40g each

2 lb/1kg cream cheese
1½ cups sugar
2 tablespoons plain flour, plus 2 teaspoons
4 whole eggs
2 egg yolks
⅓ cup double cream

1 Preheat oven to 350°F/175°C.

2 To make the base, combine wafer crumbs with the melted butter in a medium-size bowl. Mix well. Press onto bottom and sides of a 9 in/23cm springform tin. Bake for 10 minutes, remove and allow to cool.

3 To make the filling, increase oven temperature to 400°F/200°C. In a saucepan over low heat, melt caramels together with the chocolate chips and evaporated milk, stir until smooth and pour into base. Break the chocolate bars into small pieces and sprinkle over the caramel layer.

4 Beat cream cheese until smooth. Add sugar and 2 tablespoons flour and beat until smooth. Add whole eggs and egg yolks one at a time, mixing well after each addition. Blend in cream, then pour over caramel and toffee layers. Wrap outside of pan with foil.

5 Set in a large pan that has been filled with ½ in/12mm of hot water. Bake for 15 minutes, reduce oven to 230°F/110°C and bake for another hour. Remove from water, cool to room temperature then chill overnight in the refrigerator.

6 Top with whipped cream and chocolate caramel sweets to serve.

Makes 12 slices • Preparation 40 minutes, plus standing time • Cooking 1 hour 30 minutes

Plum and bitter orange cheesecake

Base
5 oz/150g gingernut biscuits
3 oz/90g butter, melted

Filling
29 oz/825g canned plums in juice
1 lb/500g cream cheese, softened
½ cup sour cream
zest of ½ orange
1 tablespoon orange juice
2–3 drops Angostura bitters
3 eggs

¾ cup caster sugar
2 tablespoons plain flour
2 tablespoons flaked almonds

Topping
¼ cup caster sugar
¼ cup unsweetened orange juice
zest of 1 orange
3–4 drops Angostura bitters
½ cup thickened cream
2 teaspoons ground cinnamon

1 Preheat oven to 300°F/150°C.

2 To make the base, line base of a 9 in/23cm springform tin with baking paper. In a food processor, process the biscuits until finely crushed, transfer to a bowl and stir in the melted butter until combined. Press firmly over the base of the tin, refrigerate while preparing filling.

4 To make the filling, drain the plums, reserving the liquid. Halve the plums and remove any stones.

5 Combine the remaining filling ingredients, except the almonds, in a large bowl. Beat with an electric mixer for about 5 minutes or until thick and smooth.

6 Pour filling over the base, top with the plums and sprinkle with almonds. Bake, uncovered, for 1 hour or until set. Cool in the tin.

7 To make the topping, place the reserved plum juice with the sugar, juice, zest and bitters in a small saucepan, bring to the boil, then simmer, uncovered, until reduced by half. Allow to cool.

8 Combine cream and cinnamon in a bowl and whisk to firm peaks.

9 Serve the cheesecake topped with the plum syrup and cinnamon cream.

Makes 12 slices • Preparation 30 minutes • Cooking 1 hour

shortbreads

Shortbread is an unleavened biscuit made from flour, sugar and butter. Unlike most cookies, shortbread is baked until white or golden in colour—never brown. Shortbread is much loved for its buttery flavour and it is this butter content that gives shortbread its distinctive crumbly texture. Although originating in Scotland, the popularity of shortbread spread across Europe. In Greece, shortbread is called *kourabiedes*, while Swedes enjoy *drömmar* or dream cookies.

Hazelnut shortbreads

8 oz/250g butter, chopped
1½ cups plain flour, sifted
1½ oz/45g hazelnuts, ground
¼ cup ground rice
¼ cup caster sugar
3½ oz/100g chocolate, melted

1 Preheat oven to 320°F/160°C.

2 Place butter, flour, hazelnuts and ground rice in a food processor and process until mixture resembles coarse breadcrumbs. Add sugar and process to combine.

3 Turn mixture onto a floured surface and knead lightly to make a pliable dough. Place dough between sheets of baking paper and roll out to ¼ in/5mm thick. Using a 2 in/5cm fluted cutter, cut out rounds of dough and place 1 in/25mm apart on buttered baking trays. Bake for 20–25 minutes or until lightly browned. Stand on baking trays for 2–3 minutes before transferring to wire racks to cool.

4 Place melted chocolate in a plastic food bag, snip off one corner and pipe lines across each biscuit before serving.

Makes 40 • Preparation 20 minutes • Cooking 25 minutes

Raspberry shortbread cakes

5 oz/150g butter
1 teaspoon vanilla extract
½ cup icing sugar
½ cup cornflour
¾ cup plain flour
4 teaspoons raspberry jam
8 frozen raspberries

1 Preheat the oven to 320°F/160°C. Melt butter in a saucepan large enough to mix all the ingredients. Remove from heat and mix in vanilla extract.

2 Sift in icing sugar, cornflour and flour and mix until combined. Fill buttered patty pans with mixture. Make a dent in the top of the mixture with your thumb. Place ½ teaspoon of raspberry jam in the dent. Top with a frozen raspberry.

3 Bake for 45 minutes or until cooked.

Makes 8 • Preparation 15 minutes • Cooking 45 minutes

Honey macadamia shortbreads

½ cup macadamias
1 cup plain flour
½ cup cornflour
¼ teaspoon salt
¼ cup caster sugar
4 oz/125g butter
2 tablespoons honey

1 Preheat oven to 400°F/200C.

2 Finely chop half the macadamias. Cut the remainder in half and put aside.

3 Sift flours, salt and sugar together. Rub in the butter until evenly dispersed, stir in the honey and chopped macadamia nuts.

4 Turn onto a lightly floured board and knead lightly. Roll out to ½ in/12mm thickness and place in the refrigerator for about 10 minutes before cutting into rounds using a 2 in/5cm fluted cutter. Place half a nut on each round.

5 Place the shortbreads on a buttered baking tray and bake in the oven for about 15 minutes, or until golden brown.

Makes 24 • Preparation 20 minutes • Cooking 15 minutes

Hazelnut and Kahlúa shortbreads

4 oz/125g butter
2 tablespoons icing sugar
2 teaspoons Kahlúa
2 tablespoons ground hazelnuts
¾ cup plain flour, sifted

1 Preheat oven to 380°F/190°C.
2 Cream butter and sugar until soft. Add liqueur and hazelnuts and mix well. Fold in sifted flour.
3 Place the mixture into a piping bag fitted with fluted tube, pipe into fancy shapes onto a lightly buttered oven tray.
4 Bake for about 12 minutes or until pale golden brown.

Makes about 30 • Preparation 10 minutes • Cooking 12 minutes

Almond and cherry shortbreads

7 oz/200g butter
3 oz/90g caster sugar
¼ teaspoon vanilla extract
8 oz/250g plain flour
3 oz/60g rice flour
¼ teaspoon baking powder
3½ oz/100g slivered almonds
3½ oz/100g glacé cherries

1 Preheat oven to 380°F/190°C.
2 Cream butter, sugar and vanilla until light and fluffy.
3 Work in sifted dry ingredients, knead well on a lightly floured surface until mixture is smooth.
4 Press into a lightly buttered lamington tin, mark into finger length pieces, prick each bar with a fork and decorate with almonds and glacé cherries.
5 Bake for about 30 minutes or until the shortbread is a light golden colour. Re-cut into fingers before serving. Store in an airtight container.

Makes 15–20 • Preparation 15 minutes • Cooking 20 minutes

Simple shortbread cookies

1 cup butter
1 cup sugar
2 cups plain flour

1 Preheat oven to 350°F/180°C.

2 Cream sugar and butter thoroughly. Add the flour and mix well. Turn out onto a lightly floured surface. Knead dough until it cracks on surface.

3 Roll out ¼ in/6mm thick and cut out with cookie cutter. Prick cookies with fork and place on unbuttered cookie sheets.

4 Bake for about 40–50 minutes, or until lightly browned.

Makes about 24 • Preparation 10 minutes • Cooking 50 minutes

Chocolate shortbread

10 oz/300g unsalted butter
1 cup caster sugar
2½ cups plain flour
5 tablespoons cocoa powder
¼ teaspoon baking soda

1 Preheat oven to 360°F/180°C.

2 Butter and line base and sides of a 8 x 12 in/20cm x 30cm lamington pan. Beat butter and sugar in a bowl until pale.

3 Sift in flour, cocoa and baking soda and beat slowly until just combined. Spread in pan and smooth with a spatula. Prick all over with a fork. Chill for 15 minutes.

4 Bake shortbread for 25 minutes or until firm to touch. While it's still hot, use a knife to score it into 12 rectangles.

5 Cool slightly, then remove from pan and cut into 12 pieces. Dust with extra cocoa before serving. Shortbread will keep for 3–4 days in an airtight container.

Makes 12 • Preparation 15 minutes • Cooking 25 minutes

Shortbread tarts with cream cheese

6½ oz/180g butter
½ cup icing sugar
1 teaspoon vanilla extract
1½ cups plain flour
2 tablespoons cornflour
⅛ teaspoon salt

Cream cheese filling
8 oz/250g cream cheese, softened
7 oz/200g sweetened condensed milk
⅓ cup freshly squeezed lemon juice
zest of 1 lemon
1 teaspoon vanilla extract
250g fresh berries or fruit of choice

1 Preheat oven to 350°F/180°C.

2 Prepare a 36-cup mini muffin tin by buttering lightly.

3 Cream the butter and sugar well. Then add the vanilla, sifted flours and salt and mix until incorporated. Do not overmix. Divide the dough into 36 even pieces and place one ball of dough in the centre of each muffin tin. Press the dough up the sides of the individual muffin tin with your fingers so there is an indentation in the centre.

4 Once filled, place the pan, with the unbaked shells, in the freezer for about 10 minutes so the shortbread can become firm. (This will help to prevent the shortbread from puffing up during baking.)

5 Bake for approximately 18–20 minutes or until lightly browned. About halfway through the baking time, lightly prick the bottom of each shortbread with a fork. Check again after another 5 minutes and prick again if needed. Once they are fully baked, remove from oven and place on a wire rack to cool. When completely cooled, remove the tarts from the tin.

6 To make the cream cheese filling, beat the cream cheese until fluffy. Add the condensed milk, lemon juice, zest, and vanilla and process until smooth. Do not over-process or the filling will be too runny. Transfer the filling to a bowl, cover, and refrigerate until serving time.

7 When ready to serve, fill the tart shells with the cream cheese filling and top with fresh berries or fruit of choice.

Makes about 36 • Preparation 35 minutes • Cooking 20 minutes

slices & squares

L ike a cross between a cake and a cookie, slices and squares are typically moist and chewy like a cake but baked flat like a cookie. Perhaps the best known (and loved) slice is the chocolate brownie, but ingredients and variations are almost limitless. From Turkish baklava to the coconut-sprinkled lamington from Australia and New Zealand, there is a slice or square to please all tastes.

Caramel squares

Shortbread base
3½ oz/100g butter
3 tablespoons sugar
2 oz/60g cornflour, sifted
¾ cup plain flour, sifted

Caramel filling
4 oz/125g butter
½ cup brown sugar
2 tablespoons honey
14 oz/400g sweetened condensed milk
1 teaspoon vanilla extract

Chocolate topping
7 oz/200g dark chocolate, melted

1 Preheat oven to 360°F/180°C. To make base, place butter and sugar in a bowl and beat until light and fluffy. Mix in cornflour and flour, turn onto a lightly floured surface and knead briefly, then press into a buttered and lined 8 x 12 in/20 x 30cm shallow cake tin and bake for 25 minutes or until firm.

2 To make filling, place butter, brown sugar and honey in a saucepan and cook over a medium heat, stirring constantly until sugar melts and ingredients are combined. Bring to the boil and simmer for 7 minutes. Beat in condensed milk and vanilla extract, pour filling over base and bake for 20 minutes longer. Set aside to cool completely. Spread melted chocolate over filling, set aside until firm, then cut into squares.

Makes 25 • Preparation 25 minutes • Cooking 45 minutes

Chocolate rum slice

1 cup self-raising flour, sifted
1 tablespoon cocoa powder, sifted
½ cup caster sugar
2½ oz/75g desiccated coconut
2½ oz/75g raisins, chopped
4 oz/125g butter, melted
1 teaspoon rum
2 tablespoons grated dark chocolate
2 eggs, lightly beaten

Chocolate icing
1 cup icing sugar
2 tablespoons cocoa powder
½ oz/15g butter, softened

1 Preheat oven to 360°F/180°C. Place flour, cocoa powder, caster sugar, coconut and raisins in a bowl and mix to combine. Stir in butter, rum, grated chocolate and eggs. Mix well.

2 Press mixture into a buttered and lined 10 in/25cm square cake tin and bake for 20–25 minutes or until firm. Allow to cool in tin.

3 To make icing, sift icing sugar and cocoa powder together into a bowl. Add butter and 1 tablespoon boiling water and beat to make icing of a spreadable consistency.

4 Turn slice onto a wire rack or plate, spread with icing and sprinkle with extra coconut. Refrigerate until icing is firm, then cut into squares.

Makes 25 • Preparation 15 minutes • Cooking 25 minutes

Cheesecake squares

2½ oz/70g butter, softened
⅓ cup firmly packed brown sugar
1 cup plain flour
½ cup sugar
8½ oz/250g cream cheese, softened
1 egg
2 tablespoons milk
1 tablespoon lemon juice
½ teaspoon vanilla extract

1 Preheat oven to 360°F/180°C.
2 In a medium bowl, blend the butter, brown sugar and flour with a fork until mixture resembles coarse breadcrumbs.
3 Put 1 cup of the mixture aside for topping. Press remaining mixture into a 8 x 8 x 2 in/20 x 20 x 5cm baking dish, bake for 15 minutes. Remove from oven and allow to cool.
4 In another bowl combine sugar and cream cheese, mixing until smooth. Thoroughly beat in egg, milk, lemon juice and vanilla. Spread over the baked base and sprinkle with remaining brown sugar mixture. Bake for 25 minutes. Cool, then chill for at least 1 hour. Cut into 12 squares.

Serves 12 • Preparation 30 minutes • Cooking 1 hour

Blueberry pecan loaf

1 cup wholemeal flour
1 cup plain flour
1½ teaspoons baking powder
1 teaspoon salt
½ teaspoon baking soda
1½ oz/45g butter
¾ cup natural yoghurt
1 tablespoon grated lemon zest
2 eggs
1 cup blueberries
1 cup chopped pecans

1 Preheat oven to 360°F/180°C.

2 Sift flours, baking powder, salt and baking soda into a processor. Add butter, process until mixture resembles course breadcrumbs.

3 Combine yoghurt, zest and eggs in a separate bowl, mix well. Add to processor and process just long enough to moisten. Add blueberries and nuts, process just long enough to combine.

4 Spoon into a buttered loaf pan, bake for about 1 hour or until a skewer comes out clean. Cool on a cake rack. Turn out and cut into ½ in/12mm slices.

Makes about 18 slices • Preparation 20 minutes • Cooking 1 hour

Cinnamon nut cigars

¼ cup walnuts, roughly chopped
1 tablespoon brown sugar
2 teaspoons ground cinnamon
6 sheets filo pastry
2 tablespoons light olive or canola oil
¼ cup pine nuts
egg white

1 Preheat oven to 360°F/180°C. Combine walnuts, sugar and cinnamon in a bowl. Layer two sheets of pastry with short side facing you. Lightly brush lower half of pastry with oil. Sprinkle with one-third of the nut mixture. Fold pastry in half. Lightly brush with oil. Sprinkle with one-third of the pine nuts. Cut into three strips lengthwise, then cut each strip in half. Roll up. Place seam side down on a buttered baking tray. Lightly brush with egg white. Repeat with remaining pastry, nut mixture and pine nuts.

2 Bake at for 10–12 minutes or until golden. Cool on a wire rack.

Makes 36 • Preparation 30 minutes • Cooking 12 minutes

Marzipan triangles

1 cup rolled oats
½ cup caster sugar
1 cup self-raising flour, sifted
¾ cup ground almonds
1 tablespoon golden syrup
½ cup canola oil
1 egg
¼ teaspoon almond extract
⅓ cup flaked almonds, to decorate

Marzipan
1 cup ground almonds
⅓ cup pure icing sugar
¼ cup caster sugar
3 teaspoons egg white (about half an egg white)
¼ teaspoon almond extract or ½ teaspoon amaretto liqueur
few drops orange blossom water or pure vanilla extract

1 To make the marzipan, sift almonds and sugars into a bowl. Add egg white, almond extract and orange water. Mix to a smooth stiff paste. Wrap in cling wrap. Chill until required.

2 Combine oats, sugar, flour and ground almonds in a bowl. Combine golden syrup, oil, egg and almond extract. Stir into oats mixture. Spread half the mixture evenly over base of a buttered and lined 8 x 12 in/20 x 30cm lamington pan.

3 Preheat oven to 360°F/180°C. Roll out marzipan and cover oats mixture. Top with remaining oats mixture. Sprinkle with chopped almonds. Press into mixture.

4 Bake for 30 minutes or until golden. Stand for 10 minutes. Cut into triangles.

Makes 42 • Preparation 30 minutes • Cooking 30 minutes

Walnut chocolate slice

4 egg whites
¼ cup sugar
4 oz/125g chocolate, melted and cooled
3 oz/90g butter, melted and cooled
1½ teaspoons vanilla extract
1 cup plain flour
¼ cup brown sugar
⅓ cup cocoa powder
2 teaspoons baking powder
½ teaspoon baking soda
⅓ cup chopped walnuts or pecans

1 Preheat oven to 380°C/190°C. Beat egg whites until soft peaks form. Gradually beat in sugar. Beat until sugar dissolves. Fold in chocolate, butter and vanilla extract.

2 Sift flour, brown sugar, cocoa, baking powder and baking soda into a large bowl. Make a well in the centre. Fold in egg whites and walnuts until just combined. Spoon into a buttered and lined 9 in/23cm square slab pan.

3 Bake for 20–25 minutes or until cooked when tested with a skewer. Cool in pan. Cut into 1½–2 in/4–5cm squares. Serve with fresh berries if desired.

Makes 25 • Preparation 20 minutes • Cooking 25 minutes

Perfect lamingtons

3 eggs
¾ cup caster sugar
¾ cup self-raising flour, sifted
¼ cup cornflour
½ oz/15g butter

Chocolate icing
2 cups icing sugar, sifted
3 tablespoons cocoa powder
¾ oz/20g tablespoons butter
2 cups shredded coconut

1 Preheat oven to 400°F/200°C.
2 Beat eggs until light with an electric mixer. Add sugar and beat until mixture is thick and creamy. Fold in sifted flours. Combine butter and 3 tablespoons boiling water and stir quickly and lightly into flour mixture.
3 Pour into a lightly buttered 7 x 11 in/18 x 28cm lamington tin and then bake for about 20 minutes.
4 Turn onto a cake stand to cool. Place in the freezer until firm but not solid. The lamingtons will cut and coat easier if half frozen.
5 Sift icing sugar and cocoa into a bowl. Blend in butter and add 4 tablespoons boiling water, mix well until smooth. Stand bowl in a pan of boiling water and stir until running consistency. Leave bowl in hot water while dipping lamingtons to keep icing the same consistency.
6 Place coconut on a sheet of paper on a flat surface.
7 Cut half-frozen cake into 12 even pieces. Hold each piece on a fork and quickly dip into warm icing, drain and toss into coconut to coat evenly. Place on a wire rack to set. Repeat with remainder.

Makes about 12 • Preparation 20 minutes • Cooking 20 minutes

Raspberry yoghurt slice

3½ oz/100g butter
1 cup plain flour
¼ cup brown sugar
¾ cup rolled oats

Topping
4 oz/125g cream cheese
¾ cup raspberry-flavoured yoghurt
1 tablespoon honey
1 teaspoon lemon juice
1 teaspoon grated lemon zest
1 tablespoon gelatine
8 oz/250g frozen raspberries
¼ cup sugar

1 Preheat oven to 360°F/180°C.

2 Blend butter and flour in a food processor with sugar until dough just comes together.
   Fold through the oats.

3 Press into the base of a buttered and lined 11 x 7 in/28 x 18cm lamington tin. Bake
   for about 15–20 minutes or until a skewer comes out clean, then allow to cool.

4 Beat the cream cheese with yoghurt and honey, add lemon juice and zest. Sprinkle
   gelatine over ¼ cup water to soften. Heat three-quarters of the thawed raspberries
   in a saucepan and add sugar and softened gelatine. Bring to the boil, stirring until
   sugar and gelatine have thoroughly dissolved. Press through a sieve, cool to egg
   white consistency. Then stir into the creamed cheese and yoghurt mixture with the
   remaining raspberries.

5 Carefully pour the yoghurt mixture over the base and refrigerate overnight. Serve
   with extra raspberries.

Makes about 15 squares • Preparation 25 minutes, plus standing time • Cooking 20 minutes

Baklava

8 oz/250g unsalted butter
14 oz/400g blanched roasted almonds, ground
1½ teaspoons ground cinnamon
½ cup caster sugar
25 oz/700g filo pastry

Syrup
3 cups caster sugar
1 cinnamon stick
1 piece of orange or lemon rind
1 tablespoon honey

1 Preheat oven to 530°F/275°C. Melt butter, set aside. Mix nuts in a bowl, with cinnamon and sugar.
2 Brush a 10 x 13 in/25 x 33cm baking tray with the butter.
3 Place one sheet of filo on bottom of dish with ends hanging over sides. Brush with melted butter and add another layer of filo. Repeat with 8 more filo sheets.
4 Sprinkle nut mixture generously over the filo. Continue layering 3 sheets of filo pastry and one layer of nuts until all nuts are used.
5 Top with 8 sheets of filo, making sure the top sheet is well buttered. Cut the top lengthwise in parallel strips.
6 Bake for 30 minutes, then reduce heat to 300°F/150°C and bake for a further hour.
7 To make the syrup. place ingredients in saucepan with 1½ cups water and bring to the boil. Reduce heat and let simmer for 10–15 minutes. Leave to cool before use. Pour cold syrup over baklava and cut into diamond shapes.

Serves 8 • Preparation 40 minutes • Cooking 1 hour 30 minutes

scones & buns

A scone is a quickbread of Scottish origin that is leavened with baking soda rather than yeast. The scone is a constituent part of the famous Devonshire tea, comprising a pot of tea, strawberry jam, whipped or clotted cream and these freshly baked goodies. Plain scones can be spiced up with ginger, currants, apple, dates, honey or even cheese.

Traditional scones

2 cups self-raising flour
2 teaspoons sugar
1 oz/30g butter, cubed
¾ cup milk
1 tablespoon lemon juice

1 Combine flour and sugar in a bowl. Add butter and lightly rub into flour using fingertips.
2 Combine milk and lemon juice in a jug.
3 Make a well in the centre of the flour. Pour in milk and, using a knife, mix to a soft, sticky dough.
4 Turn onto a floured board and knead lightly. Shape into a rectangle and cut out scones with a cutter about 1 in/25mm high.
5 Cut a piece of baking paper to fit into a heavy-based frying pan with a lid. Heat frying pan over low heat, place scones in pan, cover and cook for about 7–8 minutes each side or until golden.
6 Serve scones with butter and jam.

Makes 6–8 • Preparation 10 minutes • Cooking 16 minutes

Wholemeal scones

1 cup wholemeal self-raising flour
1 cup white self-raising flour
1 cup unprocessed bran
2 oz/60g butter
1 cup milk

1 Preheat oven to 360°F/180°C. Sift flours into a bowl, return husks from sifter to bowl, mix in bran. Rub in butter.

2 Make a well in the centre of dry ingredients, stir in enough milk to give a soft, sticky dough.

3 Turn dough onto lightly floured surface and knead lightly until smooth. Press dough out to ½ in/12mm thickness, cut into rounds with 2 in/5cm cutter.

4 Place scones into buttered slab tin, bake for 15 minutes or until golden brown.

Makes about 15 • Preparation 15 minutes • Cooking 15 minutes

Hot cross buns

3 sachets (¼ oz/7g) yeast
1 cup lukewarm milk
pinch of salt
2 tablespoons light brown
  sugar
1 teaspoon ground
  cinnamon
½ teaspoon ground nutmeg
¼ teaspoon ground allspice
2 eggs
4 cups plain flour
2 tablespoons vegetable oil
2 tablespoons mixed peel
2 tablespoons sultanas

Cross
½ cup plain flour

Glaze
½ teaspoon gelatine
2 tablespoons icing sugar
2 tablespoons warm low-fat
  milk

1 Place yeast in a large bowl. Pour in milk. Stand in warm place for 10 minutes or until frothy. Stir in salt, sugar and spices. Beat in eggs, one at a time. Stir in half the flour to make a soft dough. Beat in oil. Continue beating for 1 minute. Knead in remaining flour. Place dough in a lightly oiled bowl. Turn to coat with oil. Cover with cling wrap. Stand in a warm place for 1 hour or until doubled in size.

2 Knead dough, working in mixed peel and sultanas on a lightly floured surface. Roll into a log. Cut into 18 even-sized pieces. Shape pieces into buns. Place buns, 1 in/25mm apart, on buttered baking trays. Cover. Stand in a warm place for 20 minutes.

3 For the cross, place flour and ⅓ cup water in a bowl. Beat until smooth. Spoon cross mixture into a piping bag fitted with a small plain nozzle. Mark a cross on top each bun.

4 Preheat oven to 400°F/200°C. Bake buns for 15 minutes or until golden.

5 For the glaze, place all ingredients in a bowl. Mix until smooth. Brush warm buns with glaze.

Makes 18 • Preparation 1 hour 30 minutes • Cooking 15 minutes

Date scones

1lb/500g self-raising flour
1 teaspoon salt
2 teaspoons ground cinnamon
2 oz/60g butter
4 oz/125g chopped dates
1 oz/30g sugar
2 cups milk
1 egg
¼ cup milk

1 Preheat oven to 450°F/230°C.
2 Sift flour, salt and cinnamon then, using fingertips, rub butter into the flour mixture. Add dates and sugar. Make a well in the centre and add the milk all at once, stirring quickly and lightly to a soft dough.
3 Turn onto a lightly floured board and knead just enough to make a smooth surface. Pat into ½–¾ in/12–18mm thickness and, using a small scone cutter, cut into rounds.
4 Place on a floured baking tray. Brush tops with combined beaten egg and milk and then bake for about 10 minutes.

Makes 12–16 • Preparation 20 minutes • Cooking 10 minutes

Cheese scones

1lb/500g self-raising flour
¼ teaspoon Cayenne pepper
1 teaspoon salt
2 oz/60g butter
1 tablespoon finely chopped onion
2 oz/60g Cheddar cheese, grated
1 egg
¼ cup parsley, finely chopped
2 cups milk
1 egg, beaten
¼ cup milk

1 Preheat oven to 450°F/230°C.
2 Sift flour, pepper and salt then, using fingertips, rub butter into the flour mixture. Add onion, cheese, egg and parsley. Make a well in the centre and add the milk all at once, stirring quickly and lightly to a soft dough.
3 Turn onto a lightly floured board and knead just enough to make a smooth surface. Pat into ½–¾ in/12–18mm thickness and, using a small scone cutter, cut into rounds.
4 Place on a floured baking tray. Brush tops with combined beaten egg and milk and then bake for about 10 minutes.

Makes 12–16 • Preparation 20 minutes • Cooking 10 minutes

Honey scones

1 lb/500g self-raising white flour
1 teaspoon salt
2 oz/60g butter
1 egg
2 tablespoons honey
grated zest of 1 orange
1½ cups milk
1 egg, beaten
¼ cup milk

1 Preheat oven to 450°F/230°C.
2 Sift flours and salt then, using fingertips, rub butter into the flour mixture. Add egg, honey and zest. Make a well in the centre and add the milk all at once, stirring quickly and lightly to a soft dough.
3 Turn onto a lightly floured board and knead just enough to make a smooth surface. Pat into ½–¾ in/12–18mm thickness and, using a small scone cutter, cut into rounds.
4 Place on a floured baking tray. Brush tops with combined beaten egg and milk and then bake for about 10 minutes.

Makes 12–16 • Preparation 20 minutes • Cooking 10 minutes

Butterscotch buns

2 oz/60g butter, softened, plus 1½ oz/45g chilled
¾ cup brown sugar, packed
2 cups plain flour
2 tablespoons granulated sugar
4 teaspoons baking powder
1 teaspoon salt
¾ cup milk
⅓ cup chopped nuts

1 Preheat oven to 430°F/220°C. Cream softened butter and brown sugar together in a small bowl. Set aside.

2 In a large bowl, combine flour, sugar, baking powder and salt. Cut in chilled butter until crumbly. Make a well in the centre.

3 Pour milk into the well. Stir to make a soft dough. Knead 8–10 times. Pat or roll out on lightly floured surface to 9–10 in/23–25cm square. Spread with brown sugar mixture.

4 Sprinkle with nuts. Roll up as for jelly roll. Pinch edge to seal. Cut into 12 slices. Place on buttered 8 x 8 in/20 x 20cm pan. Bake 15–20 minutes. Invert over tray while hot.

Makes 12 • Preparation 25 minutes • Cooking 20 minutes

Apple scones

2 cups plain flour
¼ cup granulated sugar
2 teaspoons baking powder
½ teaspoon baking soda
½ teaspoon salt
1½ oz/45g butter, chilled
1 large apple, peeled and grated
½ cup milk

1 Preheat oven to 430°F/220°C. Combine flour, sugar, baking powder, baking soda and salt in a large bowl. Cut in butter until crumbly.

2 Add apple and milk. Stir to form soft dough. Turn out on lightly floured surface. Knead gently 8–10 times. Pat into two 10 in/15cm circles. Place on buttered baking sheet. Brush tops with milk. Sprinkle with sugar, then with cinnamon. Score each top into six pie-shaped wedges. Bake for 15 minutes until browned and risen. Serve warm with butter.

Makes 12 • Preparation 20 minutes • Cooking 15 minutes

Currant scones

2 cups plain flour
¼ cup granulated sugar
4 teaspoons baking powder
½ teaspoon salt
1½ oz/45g butter, chilled
½ cup currants
1 egg
½ cup milk

1 Preheat oven to 430°F/220°C. In a large bowl, combine flour, sugar, baking powder and salt. Cut in butter until crumbly. Stir in currants. Make a well in the centre.

2 In a small bowl, beat egg until frothy. Stir in milk. Pour into the well. Stir with a fork to form soft dough. Turn out on lightly floured surface. Knead 8–10 times. Divide into two equal parts. Pat each into a 6 in/15cm circle. Transfer to a buttered baking sheet.

3 Brush tops with milk and sprinkle with sugar. Score each top into six pie-shaped markings. Bake for 15 minutes until risen and browned slightly. Serve hot with butter and jam.

Makes 12 • Preparation 20 minutes • Cooking 15 minutes

Ginger scones

2 cups plain flour
1 tablespoon granulated sugar
2 teaspoons baking powder
½ teaspoon baking soda
¾ teaspoon salt
½ teaspoon groung cinnamon
½ teaspoon ground ginger
1½ oz/45g butter, chilled
1 egg
¼ cup molasses
¼ cup buttermilk or sour milk

1 Preheat oven to 430°F/220°C. Measure flour, sugar, baking powder, baking soda, salt, cinnamon and ginger into a large bowl. Stir. Cut in butter until crumbly. Make a well in the centre.

2 In a small bowl, beat egg until frothy. Mix in molasses and buttermilk. Pour into the well. Stir with fork to make a soft dough. Turn out on lightly floured surface. Knead lightly 8–10 times. Divide in half. Pat each half into a 6 in/15cm circle. Place on a buttered baking sheet.

3 Brush tops with milk. Sprinkle with sugar. Score each top into six pie-shaped wedges. Bake for 30 minutes until risen and browned. Serve hot with lots of butter.

Makes 12 • Preparation 20 minutes • Cooking 30 minutes

muffins

Whether a raspberry muffin that is as buttery as a cupcake or an oat bran muffin that is a healthy, fibre-filled treat, muffins come in all flavours, from the sweet to the savoury. Similar to a cupcake but rarely iced and seldom as sweet, muffins are a popular breakfast on the run and the perfect afternoon snack. Popular flavour additions are raspberries, dates, raisins, carrots and nuts.

Carrot and yoghurt muffins

13 oz/375g self-raising flour
½ teaspoon baking soda
1 teaspoon ground mixed spice
3 oz/90g brown sugar
1 large carrot, grated
6 oz/170g sultanas
7 oz/200g natural yoghurt
1 cup milk
1½ oz/45g butter, melted
2 eggs, lightly beaten

1 Preheat oven to 400°F/200°C. Sift flour, baking soda and mixed spice into a large bowl. Add sugar, carrot and sultanas and mix to combine.

2 Place yoghurt, milk, butter and eggs in a bowl and whisk to combine. Stir yoghurt mixture into flour mixture and mix until just combined. Spoon batter into lightly buttered muffin tins and bake for 20 minutes or until golden and cooked.

Makes 24 • Preparation 15 minutes • Cooking 20 minutes

Oat bran muffins

1¼ cups oat bran
1 cup self-raising flour
½ cup milk
2 eggs, lightly beaten
¼ cup honey
3 tablespoons safflower oil

1 Preheat oven to 360°F/180°C. Mix oat bran and flour in large bowl.
2 Blend or process milk, eggs, honey and oil until smooth, add to flour mixture. Stir until just mixed.
3 Line a muffin tin with paper cups and fill with mixture.
4 Bake for 15 minutes or until a skewer inserted in centre comes out clean.

Makes 10 • Preparation 15 minutes • Cooking 15 minutes

Raspberry muffins

1 cup wholemeal self-raising flour
1 cup white self-raising flour
½ cup bran
½ teaspoon baking soda
1 teaspoon ground ginger
¾ cup buttermilk
⅓ cup orange juice concentrate
2 eggs
⅔ cup fresh, or frozen, partly thawed, raspberries

1 Preheat oven to 360°F/150°C. Sift dry ingredients into a bowl. Return any bran to the bowl.
2 Beat together buttermilk, orange juice and eggs. Pour into dry ingredients, all at once. Add raspberries and mix until just combined – take care not to overmix. Spoon into buttered muffin pans.
3 Bake for 20–25 minutes or until cooked when tested with a skewer.

Makes 10 • Preparation 15 minutes • Cooking 25 minutes

Cheese and bacon muffins

2 cups plain flour
1 tablespoon baking powder
¼ teaspoon salt
1½ oz/45g aged Cheddar cheese, grated
4–5 bacon slices, cooked and crumbled
1 egg
1 cup milk
¼ cup olive oil

1 Preheat oven to 400°F/200°C. Put flour, baking powder, salt, cheese and bacon into a large bowl. Stir thoroughly. Make a well in the centre.
2 In a small bowl, beat egg lightly. Mix in milk and oil. Pour into the well. Stir only to moisten. Batter will be lumpy. Fill buttered muffin cups three-quarters full. Bake for 20–25 minutes. Let stand for 5 minutes. Remove from pan. Serve warm.

Makes 12 • Preparation 20 minutes • Cooking 25 minutes

Date muffins

1½ cups chopped dates
1 teaspoon baking soda
1¾ cups plain flour
1 teaspoon baking powder
½ teaspoon salt
½ cup chopped walnuts
2 eggs
¾ cup brown sugar, packed
¼ cup oil
1 teaspoon vanilla extract

1 Preheat oven to 400°F/200°C. Combine dates, ¾ cup boiling water and the baking soda in a bowl. Set aside.
2 Combine flour, baking powder, salt and nuts in a second bowl. Stir well. Set aside.
3 In a mixing bowl, beat eggs until frothy. Slowly blend in sugar, oil and vanilla. Stir in date mixture. Pour in dry ingredients from second bowl. Stir just to combine. Don't worry if the batter is lumpy. Fill buttered muffin cups three-quarters full. Bake for 20–25 minutes. Remove from pan after 5 minutes.

Makes 16 • Preparation 20 minutes • Cooking 25 minutes

Peanut butter muffins

1½ cups plain flour
¼ cup granulated sugar
1 tablespoon baking powder
½ teaspoon salt
1 cup rolled oats
1 cup milk
1 egg
½ cup smooth peanut butter
¼ cup oil

1 Preheat oven to 400°F/200°C. Combine flour, sugar, baking powder and salt in a large bowl. Stir to mix. Make a well in the centre.
2 Combine oats with milk in medium bowl.
3 Add egg and peanut butter to oats. Beat with spoon to mix well. Add oil and stir. Pour into well. Stir just enough to moisten. Batter will be lumpy. Fill buttered muffin cups three-quarters full. Bake for 15–20 minutes. Wait 5 minutes for easier removal of muffins. Serve warm.

Makes 12 • Preparation 20 minutes • Cooking 20 minutes

Pumpkin muffins

1½ cups plain flour
1 teaspoon baking powder
1 teaspoon baking soda
½ teaspoon salt
½ teaspoon ground cinnamon
½ teaspoon ground nutmeg
½ teaspoon ground ginger
½ cup raisins
1 egg
¼ cup granulated sugar
⅓ cup olive oil
1 cup cooked pumpkin
½ cup milk

1   Preheat oven to 400°F/200°C. Combine flour, baking powder, baking soda, salt, cinnamon, nutmeg, ginger and raisins in a large bowl. Stir thoroughly. Make a well in the centre.

2   In a small bowl, beat egg until frothy. Mix in sugar, oil, pumpkin and milk. Pour into well. Stir only to moisten. Batter will be lumpy. Fill buttered muffin cups three-quarters full. Bake for 15–20 minutes. Let stand 5 minutes. Remove from pan. Serve warm. Dust with icing sugar.

Makes 12 • Preparation 25 minutes • Cooking 20 minutes

Berry crumble muffins

1 cup self-raising flour, sifted
1 cup plain flour, sifted
1 teaspoon baking powder
½ cup brown sugar
¾ cup milk
¼ cup canola oil
2 eggs, lightly beaten
1 cup frozen mixed berries

Crumble topping
2 tablespoons plain flour
2 tablespoons brown sugar
1 oz/30g butter, cut into cubes

1 Preheat oven to 360°F/180C°C. Butter 12 medium muffin tins.

2 In a medium bowl sift together the flours and baking powder and stir in the sugar.

3 In a separate bowl, mix the milk, oil and eggs together. Make a well in the centre of the dry ingredients and pour in the milk mixture.

4 Add the berries and mix until just combined.

5 To make the crumble topping, place the flour and butter in a medium bowl and rub in the butter with your fingertips until the mixture resembles breadcrumbs. Stir in the sugar and set aside.

6 Spoon the dough into muffin tins and sprinkle with the crumble mixture. Bake for 20–25 minutes or until muffins are cooked when tested with skewer. Turn onto wire racks to cool.

Makes 12 • Preparation 20 minutes • Cooking 25 minutes

Raisin muffins

1½ cups plain flour, sifted
2 teaspoons baking powder
½ teaspoon salt
¼ cup raw sugar
1 cup seeded raisins
¾ cup milk
1 egg
1¼ oz/45g butter, melted

1 Preheat oven to 360°F/180C°C. Butter 12 medium muffin tins.

2 In a medium bowl, sift together flour, baking powder, salt and sugar. Mix in raisins.

3 Place egg, milk and butter in a small bowl and whisk to combine. Pour milk mixture into dry ingredients and mix with a fork until ingredients are just combined, do not over-mix.

4 Spoon mixture into 12 buttered muffin tins. Bake for 20–25 minutes or until muffins are cooked when tested with a skewer. Turn onto wire racks to cool.

Makes 12 • Preparation 20 minutes • Cooking 25 minutes

Carrot muffins

1½ cups plain flour, sifted
2 teaspoons baking powder
½ teaspoon salt
3 tablespoons sugar
1 teaspoon ground cinnamon
1 teaspoon ground nutmeg
1 cup grated carrot
¼ cup currants
1 egg
½ cup milk
2½ oz/75g butter, melted

1　Preheat oven to 360°F/180C°C. Butter 12 medium muffin tins.

2　In a medium bowl, sift together flour, baking powder, salt, sugar and spices. Mix in grated carrot and currants.

3　Place egg, milk and butter in a small bowl and whisk to combine. Pour milk mixture into dry ingredients and mix with a fork until ingredients are just combined, do not over-mix.

4　Spoon mixture into 12 buttered muffin tins. Bake for 20–25 minutes or until muffins are cooked when tested with a skewer. Turn onto wire racks to cool.

Makes 12 • Preparation 20 minutes • Cooking 25 minutes

cupcakes

Cupcakes, fairy cakes or patty cakes are individual cakes made to serve one person. Baked in batches of several cakes in a cupcake pan or individual paper cases, these mini cakes are the mainstay of children's parties, but also loved by the young at heart. A distinctive feature of the cupcake is its icing and decorations, from the simple sprinkle to the creation of ornate butterfly wings from the trimmed top of the cupcake itself.

Chocolate fruity cupcakes

4 oz/125g butter
½ cup sugar
2 eggs
1 cup sultanas
3 oz/90g glacé cherries, chopped
¼ cup chocolate chips, chopped
1½ cups self-raising flour
¼ cup cocoa powder
½ cup milk

Chocolate icing
1½ cups icing sugar
1 tablespoon cocoa powder
1 teaspoon melted butter
2 tablespoons milk

1 Preheat oven to 360°F/180°C.
2 Cream butter and sugar until light and fluffy, add eggs, one at a time, beating well after each addition.
3 Fold in sultanas, chopped cherries and chocolate then flour, cocoa and milk alternately.
4 Drop teaspoons of mixture into well-buttered deep patty pans or paper patty cases. Bake for about 15 minutes
5 Sift icing sugar and cocoa into a small basin, add melted butter and milk and beat until smooth.
6 Spread chocolate icing over top of cakes while hot, then top with extra sultanas, cherries and chocolate to garnish.

Makes about 30 • Preparation 20 minutes • Cooking 15 minutes

Ladybird cupcakes

9 oz/270g butter, softened
1 cup caster sugar
3 eggs
½ cup buttermilk
1½ cups self-raising flour, sifted
1 teaspoon vanilla extract

Topping
1½ cups icing sugar
3 oz/90g butter, softened
6 drops vanilla extract
red food colouring
18 mini white marshmallows
liquorice strap

1 Preheat the oven to 320°F/160°C. Line a 12-cup muffin tin with cupcake papers.

2 Using an electric mixer, cream the butter and sugar, until light and fluffy. Add the eggs one at a time, beating well after each addition.

3 Add buttermilk, flour and vanilla extract and stir to combine. Beat with an electric mixer until light and creamy.

4 Divide the mixture evenly between the cupcake papers. Bake for about 20 minutes, until risen and firm to the touch. Allow to cool for a few minutes, then transfer to a wire rack. Allow to cool fully before icing.

5 To make the topping, combine icing sugar, butter and vanilla extract and stir with a spoon until mixed together and mixture is light and fluffy. Tint the icing to the required shade of red with the food colouring, then spread evenly onto the cupcakes, making a nice hump for the ladybirds back.

6 Cut the liquorice into thin strips and make lines down the centre of each cake for the wings. Cut a cross section of marshmallow with scissors and cut a half circle of liquorice for the head and spots for the back. Place this on the half circle of liquorice to make the face. Place the liquorice spots on the back to make the ladybird spots and small pieces of liquorice on the marshmallows for the eyes.

Makes about 18 • Preparation 40 minutes • Cooking 20 minutes

Baby Violet cupcakes

3 eggs
3 oz/90g butter, softened
1 cup caster sugar
½ cup milk
1½ cups self-raising flour, sifted
1 teaspoon vanilla extract

Topping
1½ cups icing sugar
3 oz/90g butter, softened
6 drops purple food colouring
3 teaspoons coloured sugar sprinkles
12 miniature baby rattle toys

1 Preheat the oven to 320°F/160°C. Line a 12-cupcake pan with cupcake papers. In a medium-sized bowl, lightly beat the eggs, add butter and sugar, then mix until light and fluffy.

2 Add milk, flour and vanilla, and stir to combine. Beat with an electric mixer for 2 minutes, until light and creamy.

3 Divide the mixture evenly between the cake papers. Bake for 18–20 minutes until risen and firm to touch. Allow to cool for a few minutes and then transfer to a wire rack. Allow to cool fully before icing.

4 To make the topping, thoroughly combine the topping ingredients with 1 tablespoon water. Using the back of a teaspoon, apply the topping to cupcakes. Top with purple sugar sprinkles and a novelty toy.

Makes 12 • Preparation 12 minutes • Cooking 20 minutes

Vanilla sprinkles cupcakes

3 eggs
1 cup butter, softened
1 cup caster sugar
½ cup milk
1½ cups self-raising flour, sifted
1 teaspoon vanilla extract
1 teaspoon cocoa powder

Topping
½ cup icing sugar
sprinkles (or 100s & 1000s)

1 Preheat the oven to 320°F/160°C. Line a 12-cupcake pan with cupcake papers. In a
   medium-sized bowl, lightly beat the eggs, add butter and sugar, then mix until light
   and fluffy.

2 Add milk, flour and vanilla, and stir to combine. Beat with an electric mixer for
   2 minutes, until light and creamy.

3 Divide the mixture in half, and add the vanilla to one half and cocoa powder to the
   other, then divide evenly between the cake papers. Bake for 18–20 minutes until
   risen and firm to touch. Allow to cool for a few minutes and then transfer to a wire
   rack. Allow to cool fully before icing.

4 To make the topping, combine icing sugar and ¾ tablespoon hot water in a small
   bowl, and mix with a wooden spoon. Spoon onto cupcakes. Tip sprinkles onto a
   small plate and gently press each cupcake into the sprinkles.

Makes 12 • Preparation 12 minutes • Cooking 20 minutes

Cherry-top cupcakes

3 eggs
1 cup butter, softened
1 cup caster sugar
½ cup milk
1½ cups self-raising flour, sifted
1 teaspoon vanilla extract
1 tablespoon cocoa powder

Topping
1 cup dark chocolate drops
½ oz/15g butter, at room temperature
⅓ cup thickened cream
6 glacé cherries, halved

1 Preheat the oven to 320°F/160°C. Line a 12-cupcake pan with cupcake papers. In a medium-sized bowl, lightly beat the eggs, add butter and sugar, then mix until light and fluffy.

2 Add milk, flour, vanilla and cocoa powder, and stir to combine. Beat with an electric mixer for 2 minutes, until light and creamy.

3 Divide the mixture evenly between the cupcake cases. Bake for 18–20 minutes until risen and firm to touch. Allow to cool for a few minutes and then transfer to a wire rack. Allow to cool fully before icing.

4 To make the topping, combine the chocolate and butter in a medium-sized saucepan over a medium heat. As the mixture begins to melt, reduce heat to low, stirring constantly, until melted. Remove from heat, add cream, and stir. Rest for 10 minutes – the mixture will be firm and velvety in consistency.

5 Spoon into a piping bag with a broad nozzle, and pipe onto cupcakes in a spiral. Top with cherry pieces.

Makes 12 • Preparation 12 minutes • Cooking 20 minutes

Toffee meringue crunch cupcakes

3 eggs
6 oz/180g butter, softened
1 cup caster sugar
½ cup milk
2 cups self-raising flour, sifted

1 teaspoon vanilla extract
½ cup peanuts, crushed

Butter cream topping
1 cup icing sugar
6 oz/180g butter, at room temperature

Meringue topping
3 egg whites
¼ teaspoon cream of tartar
½ cup sugar

Toffee
½ caster sugar

1 Preheat the oven to 320°F/160°C. Line a 12-cupcake pan with cupcake papers. In a medium-sized bowl, lightly beat the eggs, add butter and sugar, then mix until light and fluffy.

2 Add milk, flour and vanilla, and stir to combine. Beat with an electric mixer for 2 minutes, until light and creamy. Fold in crushed peanuts.

3 Divide the mixture evenly between the cake papers. Bake for 18–20 minutes until risen and firm to touch. Allow to cool for a few minutes and then transfer to a wire rack. Allow to cool fully before icing.

4 To make the butter cream topping, combine half the icing sugar and butter, mix with a wooden spoon, add remaining sugar and butter and beat with the spoon until light and fluffy. Spread onto cupcakes.

5 To make the meringue topping, create a double boiler by bringing 2 cups of water to the boil in a medium-sized saucepan, and reduce heat slightly. Place a glass bowl into the saucepan that is large enough to fit into the pan while still resting on the top rim.

6 Add the egg whites to the hot bowl and whisk until foaming. Add cream of tartar and whisk until fluffy. Pour in the sugar slowly in one stream, whisking constantly to form stiff peaks.

7 Spread mixture onto a baking sheet and lightly brown under the grill for 1–2 minutes. Place in the oven for 3 minutes, then open the oven door slightly and leave meringue for a further 3 minutes.

8 To make the toffee, place ½ cup caster sugar evenly on a greaseproof paper-lined baking tray, and bake at 400°F/200°C for approximately 25 minutes until toffee consistency forms. Cool until hardened.

9 Crumble the meringue topping onto the cupcakes, then crumble the toffee on top.

Makes 12 • Preparation 12 minutes • Cooking 30 minutes

Sticky date cupcakes

2 eggs
4½ oz/135g butter, at room temperature
¾ cup caster sugar
1 cup self-raising flour, sifted
400g dates, chopped
2 teaspoons instant coffee powder
1 teaspoon baking soda
1 teaspoon vanilla extract
1 cup ground almond flour
½ cup walnuts, finely chopped

Topping
1 cup packed light-brown sugar
2 oz/60g unsalted butter
1 teaspoon vanilla extract
1½ oz/45g dates

1 Preheat the oven to 320°F/160°C. Line a 12-cupcake pan with cupcake papers. In a medium-sized bowl, lightly beat the eggs, add butter and sugar, then mix until light and fluffy.

2 Add ¾ cup water and the flour, and stir to combine. Add remaining cupcake ingredients. Mix with a wooden spoon for 2 minutes, until light and creamy.

3 Divide the mixture evenly between the cake papers. Bake for 18–20 minutes until risen and firm to touch. Allow to cool for a few minutes and then transfer to a wire rack. Allow to cool fully before icing.

4 To make the topping, combine sugar, butter, vanilla and 2 tablespoon water in a saucepan. Bring to a simmer over medium-low heat, stirring constantly. Without stirring again, simmer for 1 minute. Remove from heat, allow to cool and spoon onto cakes. Top each cupcake with a date and more topping. Heat the top of each cupcake with a blowtorch, being careful not to scorch the paper or the dates.

Makes 12 • Preparation 12 minutes • Cooking 20 minutes

Caramel nougat cupcakes

3 eggs
6 oz/180g butter, softened
1 cup caster sugar
½ cup milk
1½ cups self-raising flour
1 teaspoon vanilla extract

Topping
1 cup icing sugar
6 oz/180g butter, room temperature
100g nougat, chopped

1 Preheat the oven to 320°F/160°C. Line a 12-cupcake pan with cupcake papers. In a
   medium-sized bowl, lightly beat the eggs, add butter and sugar, then mix until light
   and fluffy.
2 Add milk, flour and vanilla, and stir to combine. Beat with an electric mixer for
   2 minutes, until light and creamy.
3 Divide the mixture evenly between the cake papers. Bake for 18–20 minutes until
   risen and firm to touch. Allow to cool for a few minutes and then transfer to a wire
   rack. Allow to cool fully before icing.
4 To make the topping, combine icing sugar and butter in a small bowl, mix, and add
   chopped nougat. Stir and spoon onto cupcakes in mounds.

Makes 12 • Preparation 12 minutes • Cooking 20 minutes

Pistachio zinger cupcake

3 eggs
6 oz/180g butter, softened
1 cup caster sugar
½ cup yoghurt
2 cups self-raising flour, sifted
1 teaspoon vanilla extract
1 zucchini, grated
juice of ½ a lime
zest of 1 lime
½ cup pistachios

Topping
1 cup icing sugar
6 oz/180g butter, room temperature
zest of 1 lime
½ cup pistachios

1 Preheat the oven to 320°F/160°C. Line a 12-cupcake pan with cupcake papers. In a medium-sized bowl, lightly beat the eggs, add butter and sugar, then mix until light and fluffy.

2 Add yoghurt, flour and vanilla, and stir to combine. Beat with an electric mixer for 2 minutes, until light and creamy. Add zucchini, lime juice, zest and pistachios and mix through.

3 Divide the mixture evenly between the cake papers. Bake for 18–20 minutes until risen and firm to touch. Allow to cool for a few minutes and then transfer to a wire rack. Allow to cool fully before icing.

4 To make the topping, combine half the icing sugar and butter, mix with a wooden spoon, then add remaining icing sugar and butter, and beat with the spoon until light and fluffy. Add lime zest and half of the pistachios and mix through.

5 Apply icing to cupcakes with the back of a spoon or a small spatula, and sprinkle each cake with a few of the remaining nuts.

Makes 12 • Preparation 12 minutes • Cooking 20 minutes

Hazelnut express

3 eggs
6 oz/180g butter, softened
1 cup caster sugar
½ cup milk
1 cup self-raising flour, sifted
¼ teaspoon baking powder
½ cup hazelnut meal
½ cup hazelnuts, chopped
½ cup cocoa powder
2 tablespoons instant coffee powder

Topping
1 cup icing sugar
3 oz/90g unsalted butter
1 tablespoon hazelnut liqueur
12 coffee beans

1 Preheat the oven to 320°F/160°C. Line a 12-cupcake pan with cupcake papers. In a medium-sized bowl, lightly beat the eggs, add butter and sugar, then mix until light and fluffy.

2 Add milk and flour, and stir to combine. Add remaining cupcake ingredients. Mix with a wooden spoon for 2 minutes, until light and creamy.

3 Divide the mixture evenly between the cake papers. Bake for 18–20 minutes until risen and firm to touch. Allow to cool for a few minutes and then transfer to a wire rack. Allow to cool fully before icing.

4 To make the topping, combine all topping ingredients except for coffee beans in a small bowl, mix with a wooden spoon, and spoon onto cupcakes. Decorate each cake with a coffee bean.

Makes 12 • Preparation 12 minutes • Cooking 20 minutes

Index

Almond and cherry shortbreads	158	Cinnamon cookies	49
Almond biscotti	54	Cinnamon nut cigars	176
Almond cheesecake	131	Citrus delicious pudding	109
Apple and berry crumble	101	Coconut poori	32
Apple and rhubarb crumble	105	Cornish pasties	82
Apple scones	205	Country cornbread	15
Baby Violet cupcakes	238	Croissants	20
Baked fresh dates and apples	110	Currant scones	206
Baklava	187	Date muffins	220
Basil beer bread	19	Date scones	197
Beef and mushroom pie	86	Fougasse Provençale	43
Berry crumble muffins	227	French baguettes	24
Blueberry pecan loaf	175	French olive ladder bread	23
Brandied plum clafouti	98	French sourdough with caramelised onions	40
Butter cookies	65	Fresh fruit tartlets	78
Butterscotch buns	202	Fruit mince pies	81
Caramel nougat cupcakes	249	Ginger biscuits	61
Caramel squares	168	Ginger honey cheesecake	143
Carrot and yoghurt muffins	212	Ginger scones	209
Carrot muffins	231	Ginger snaps	62
Chapatis	36	Grand Marnier soufflé	113
Cheese and bacon muffins	219	Hazelnut and Kahlúa shortbreads	157
Cheese scones	198	Hazelnut express	253
Cheesecake squares	172	Hazelnut macaroons	58
Cherry-top cupcakes	242	Hazelnut raspberry cheesecake	136
Chocolate caramel cheesecake	132	Hazelnut shortbreads	150
Chocolate fruity cupcakes	234	Herbed beer bread	31
Chocolate rum slice	171	Holiday spice bread	39
Chocolate shortbread	162	Honey macadamia shortbreads	154

Honey scones	201
Hot cross buns	194
Individual meat pies	85
Ladybird cupcakes	237
Marzipan triangles	179
Mini passionfruit cheesecake	139
Naan bread	12
Oat bran muffins	215
Oatmeal biscuits	53
Old English pork pie	89
Orange and lime cheesecake	128
Orange poppy seed cake	120
Papaya lime cheesecake	140
Peanut butter and honey cookies	57
Peanut butter muffins	223
Pear and fig flan	70
Pear upside down pudding	106
Pecan and almond cakes	123
Pecan crispies	50
Perfect lamingtons	183
Pide	28
Pistachio oat bran biscuits	66
Pistachio zinger cupcake	250
Plum and bitter orange cheesecake	147
Potato naan	35
Potato, egg and leek pies	90
Pumpkin muffins	224
Raisin muffins	228
Raspberry and hazelnut tarts	74
Raspberry chocolate truffle cakes	116

Raspberry muffins	216
Raspberry shortbread cakes	153
Raspberry yoghurt slice	184
Rhubarb and apple tart	73
Rhubarb soufflé	97
Shortbread tarts with cream cheese	165
Simple shortbread cookies	161
Soda bread	16
Spiced apple cake	119
Spicy pumpkin pie	77
Sticky date cupcakes	246
Sultana and bourbon cheesecake	135
Sweet cinnamon bows	46
Sweet pumpkin coyotas	102
The perfect pavlova	94
Toffee cheesecake	144
Toffee meringue crunch cupcakes	245
Traditional scones	190
Vanilla sprinkles cupcakes	241
Victoria sandwich cake	124
Walnut chocolate slice	180
Wholemeal damper	27
Wholemeal scones	193